From Mindfulness To Heartfulness

Transforming Self And Society With Compassion

Stephen Murphy-Shigematsu

16pt

Copyright Page from the Original Book

From Mindfulness to Heartfulness

Copyright © 2018 by Stephen Murphy-Shigematsu

All rights reserved. No part of this publication may be reproduced, distributed, or transmitted in any form or by any means, including photocopying, recording, or other electronic or mechanical methods, without the prior written permission of the publisher, except in the case of brief quotations embodied in critical reviews and certain other noncommercial uses permitted by copyright law. For permission requests, write to the publisher, addressed "Attention: Permissions Coordinator," at the address below.

Berrett-Koehler Publishers, Inc.
1333 Broadway, Suite 1000
Oakland, CA 94612-1921
Tel: (510) 817-2277, Fax: (510) 817-2278
www.bkconnection.com

Ordering information for print editions

Quantity sales. Special discounts are available on quantity purchases by corporations, associations, and others. For details, contact the "Special Sales Department" at the Berrett-Koehler address above.

Individual sales. Berrett-Koehler publications are available through most bookstores. They can also be ordered directly from Berrett-Koehler: Tel: (800) 929-2929; Fax: (802) 864-7626; www.bkconnection.com

Orders for college textbook/course adoption use. Please contact Berrett-Koehler: Tel: (800) 929-2929; Fax: (802) 864-7626.

Distributed to the U.S. trade and internationally by Penguin Random House Publisher Services.

Berrett-Koehler and the BK logo are registered trademarks of Berrett-Koehler Publishers, Inc.

First Edition
Paperback print edition ISBN 978-1-5230-9455-4
PDF e-book ISBN 978-1-5230-9456-1
IDPF e-book ISBN 978-1-5230-9457-8

2018-1

Cover design: Dan Tesser. Book interior production and design: VJB/Scribe.

Copyediting: Mark Woodworth. Proofreader: Nancy Bell. Index: Susan Clements.

TABLE OF CONTENTS

Praise for From Mindfulness to Heartfulness	i
Preface	xiv
INTRODUCTION: HEARTFULNESS	xxiv
1: BEGINNER'S MIND	1
2: VULNERABILITY	40
3: AUTHENTICITY	79
4: CONNECTEDNESS	114
5: LISTENING	151
6: ACCEPTANCE	188
7: GRATITUDE	226
8: SERVICE	263
Notes	303
Acknowledgments	327
About the Author	329
Index	339

Praise for From Mindfulness to Heartfulness

"*From Mindfulness to Heartfulness* is a rare gem—beautifully written, deeply engaging, and filled with valuable and authentic teachings about practical and spiritual paths toward balance and understanding. As Murphy-Shigematsu embraces his vulnerability, he opens up to and reflects upon his life stories, and that can inspire us to do the same—encouraging us toward knowledge and understanding. Just what is needed to bring the increasingly popular mindfulness approach back to its reality core—the blending of heartfulness with mindfulness."

—Richard Katz, PhD, Professor Emeritus, First Nations University of Canada, and author of *Indigenous Healing Psychology*

"Through tender teaching stories and an insightful narrative, Stephen

Murphy-Shigematsu shows us the ways we can weave together mindfulness and compassion into what he terms *heartfulness*. As master educator, he leads us through the stages of heartfulness from vulnerability and connectedness to acceptance and gratitude. This is an important book. I heartfully recommend it to all who want to join their own personal journey of self-discovery to selfless service and the care for others."

—**Arthur Zajonc, Professor of Physics Emeritus, Amherst College, and former President, Mind and Life Institute**

"This book has the potential for radical change in the way we live together, and I loved reading it! Stephen Murphy-Shigematsu takes us beyond mindfulness as it is often currently taught—as an instrument for cognitive changes like focus, attention, or stress relief—to the truths of the gentle, appreciative, nurturing heart. He shows us through stories and practices how to expand our contemplative lives from being self-focused to being inclusive, connected, compassionate, and responsible. Immense heartfulness shines through every story he tells, drawing on experiences from teaching children and college students to being with his dying grandmother to his own bi racial childhood. Each story is a jewel, opening the heart. He connects heartfulness to social justice, leadership, and education and offers simple, direct instructions for seven heartful practices."

—Mirabai Bush, Senior Fellow, The Center for Contemplative Mind in Society, and author of *Compassion in Action* (with Ram Dass) and *Contemplative Practices in Higher Education* (with Daniel Barbezat)

"This powerful book is full of love and intimate wisdom. Full of rich stories and deep guidance, it is also a map of the human heart and the best in all of us."

—Roshi Joan Halifax, PhD, Abbot, Upaya Zen Center

"Resonant with Stephen's kindness, heartfulness, and wisdom and filled with

excellent exercises and practical guides, this lovely volume will be a friend and guide to all those intent on creating and sustaining thriving lives, workplaces, relationships, and communities."
—**Dan Barbezat, Professor of Economics, Amherst College**

"A profound and wise book written by a respected colleague and friend ... this book humbly reminds us that mindfulness without the heart is lacking and shows the way to live our lives with awareness, compassion, and responsibility."
—**Frederic Luskin PhD, cofounder of LifeWorks, Stanford University, and author of** *Forgive for Good*

"I couldn't put this book down! Dr. Stephen Murphy-Shigematsu's *From Mindfulness to Heartfulness* is a profound exploration in heartful connection with ourselves and others. Through moving storytelling, Murphy-Shigematsu offers several integral components to cultivating a heartful way of being. Drawing on examples from his college teaching, his many talks to corporations and public audiences, and vulnerable moments from his own life, Murphy-Shigematsu illustrates what this heartful journey might look like—*he is in it with us.* He models the vulnerability heartfulness calls for, exploring the fraught experience of living a biracial identity in the racial contexts of both the United States and Japan. The insights that result offer a model of compassionate transformation that are applicable in a variety of contexts, including social justice, education, health care, corporations, and community work.

"This book is accessible, mesmerizing, and practical, offering both deep insights to ponder for days and practical tips to enact right now. It promises to become a classic mindfulness resource."

—Beth Berila, PhD, RYT 500, Director, Women's Studies Program, St. Cloud State University

"Master listener Dr. Murphy-Shigematsu demonstrates his

attunement to the needs of a multicultural and stress-filled world by distilling wisdom stories from a range of perspectives to illuminate the holistic dynamics of heartfulness. His intimate stories exemplify how to live with heartfulness. They inspire and empower us to heal through a mindful awareness that plumbs the personally and socially transformative power of heartfulness."
—**Paula Arai, PhD, author of *Women Living Zen* and *Bringing Zen Home***

"The focus is not on how you can reduce stress through mindfulness but on teachings that sensitively and carefully show us a valuable way that humans can live good lives."
—**Roshi Nanrei Yokota, Enkaku-ji Zen Temple Master**

"A moving testament and sharing of the lessons learned from the author's grandmother, the daughter of a samurai, who taught him the art of living with heartfulness. The book is the distillation of many years of searching for authenticity, making peace with his vulnerabilities, exploring his connectedness with others, and finding his unique purpose in life. I am deeply moved by his stories of integrating the American and Japanese values and his insights on achieving mindfulness. The exercises in the book are a helpful guide for us to find our own meaning in our lives."

—Reiko Homma-True, Professor Emerita, Alliant International University

"Murphy-Shigematsu, through vivid and insightful storytelling, shows how our connections to our ethnic and cultural heritage can guide and enrich our search for both enlightenment and social justice. The beautiful stories here bring vivid color to the practice of mindfulness that may seem like a world of whiteness in which race and culture are dismissed as worldly distractions on the spiritual journey."

—Satsuki Ina, PhD, filmmaker, psychotherapist, and community activist

"Dr. Murphy-Shigematsu's book offers an insightful new perspective on practicing mindfulness to cultivate heartful interconnections instead of just using it for stress reduction. This book is a timely and a much-needed intervention/response to corporate mindfulness. Using cultural and personal stories, Dr. Murphy-Shigematsu offers a moving narrative account of cultivating compassionate wisdom by opening our heart to listen to stories in and around our lives. The book is moving, wonderful, and heartfelt and an excellent guide to fully engaging in life with our heart."

—Ramaswami Mahalingam, Professor of Psychology, University of Michigan, Ann Arbor

"Wisdom of the heart. Murphy-Shigematsu's gentle storytelling deftly illustrates a compassionate centering to the mindfulness movement sweeping across the country. In sharing the wisdom of his grandmother, he reminds us that outward-focused love and compassion are the complements

to inward-focused peace and clarity. Significantly, this recentering is developed through stories that are cross-cultural and intercultural, illustrating how heartfulness provides compassionate pathways for navigating increasingly diverse societies. A valuable book."
—**anthony lising antonio,
Associate Professor of
Education, Stanford University**

"In a society where supposed 'intelligence' is measured by a person's ability to analyze and compute, Stephen Murphy-Shigematsu reminds us that the depth of our humanity is more than a number, an algorithm, or a test score. In a powerful story only he can tell, Stephen shows us a workable path that crosses cultures, boundaries, and identities that stitches a broken world back together."
—**Jeremy Hunter, PhD, Founding Director, Executive Mind Leadership Institute, Peter F. Drucker and Masatoshi Ito Graduate School of Management**

"Mindfulness has become a contemporary cliché, all too often taken far from its roots to be practiced in ways that exemplify the very problems of solipsism and disregard it was meant to transform. Encouraging us instead toward heartfulness, Stephen Murphy-Shigematsu returns us to the importance of presence, empathy, and compassion. With humor, humility, and vulnerability, he guides us back toward thinking of how we might live, work, and act together in diverse and inclusive communities."

—Jeff Chang, author of *We Gon' Be Alright*

"Murphy-Shigematsu is a master of storytelling. By artfully weaving together personal threads of his bicultural upbringing with accessible spiritual practices informed by Buddhism and modern psychotherapy, he becomes our friend and Sherpa, guiding us to reaching our highest human potential. Heartfulness is a life-changing philosophy, intended to heal not only individuals but communities at large.

Reading this book will make you a better person."
—**Isabel Stenzel Byrnes, bereavement counselor and author of** *The Power of Two*

To my grandmother

Preface

"She waited for you," the priest told me. I believe she did.

It had been a long trip to get there and my Grandmother Mitsu had been on a much longer journey in this world. She was 111, though the priest pronounced her 113 by the Buddhist way of counting age. Her old body had finally broken down and I couldn't just let her go, so I went to Japan.

With a heavy feeling that this was my last time to see her, I made the long trip across the ocean. When I finally arrived in her room and saw her tiny body, my heart sank, as she appeared to be unconscious. I stared at her for a while, thinking that I had come for nothing. But when I spoke to her, "Grandma," she opened her eyes and looked into mine. "It's me," I said. "Stephen." She recognized me and her eyes closed. We did this a few more times before she appeared to fall into a deep sleep. Wanting to get away for a moment from the enormity of the situation, I went outside into the falling darkness, wandering through neighborhoods filled with sights, sounds, and scents of home—fish grilling, television news blaring, students bicycling home.

When I returned, her condition had markedly changed. The nurse said that she was rejecting food and even water. The doctor was called and after examining her told me that she was "nearing the mountaintop"—an unfamiliar expression but one I instantly understood. He left the room and I waited alone by her side. The only sound was the rhythm of her harsh breathing. After a few hours, I grew weary and fell asleep.

A short while later I awoke to a strange silence. I knew that it was over. Her long time in this world had ended. As I gazed at the lifeless body, I sensed that she was no longer there.

The funeral ended with family members placing flowers on Grandmother's body, especially around her face, before the coffin was closed. We then moved to the crematorium. There we watched as the body was rolled into the oven and the switch turned on. None of this was horrifying. I sensed no life in the body, no grandmother. Whatever form she was now in, it clearly was not attached to that body.

My mother could not make the trip to Japan, so as the only grandson I was the designated person in charge of the ceremonies. Many people came up to me and reminded me what a big heart Grandmother had. I saw how she had always been so attentive and aware of the needs of others, so compassionate in giving, and so responsible in serving the interests of the family and community.

When I was leaving for the airport, the priest told me once again, "She waited for you. It is good you came. It gave her peace and she was able to let go."

It's still a mystery that she waited for me. Maybe grandmother wanted to give me the final message that everything was all right. She was okay. I would be okay. We were connected so deeply. When I was a lost young man in my twenties, I felt called to be by her side and lived with her in the

Japanese countryside as I regained my strength to go on. Grandmother cared for me and taught me many things about life. I absorbed some of her tremendous life energy. She taught me about the beauty of a way of being in which I needed to accept who I was, be grateful for it, and responsibly do what I could with what I had. My life was transformed in what my awed father called "a metamorphosis!"

Grandmother's passing birthed a renewed sense of being called back home; to connect with my heritage; to remember who I am. Reflecting on her life, I remember how much Grandmother lived with her heart. At the funeral, so many people spoke of her with the word *kokoro,* expressing a broad sense of wholeness, with heart, mind, and spirit. Her being expressed mindfulness, compassion, and responsibility, and the closest word in English that describes her is "heartfulness."

It has become clear to me that for many years I have been teaching what I learned from my grandmother about the art of living with heartfulness. At first, I called it storytelling, or narrative. Then it became emotional intelligence. More recently it was labeled *mindfulness.* All these words describe a way of living that is heart-centered, beyond a focus on mind. I saw that I had been teaching about heartfulness in diverse contexts, without calling it by that word.

The responses to a heartfulness approach tell me that it has meaning in people's lives. The training that I do with American, Japanese, and Singaporean government employees is described as "staying in your heart" rather than "disappearing from your brain." College and high school students call my classes transformative, with life lessons that remain with them. Doctors, counselors, and coaches alike declare that heartful courses empower them with both empathy and respect.

Heartened by this response, I am propelled by the urgency of doing something, no matter how small, to heal personal suffering and to revive our sick society and destructive world. If we are awake and aware, we know that we live in a dangerous time in which our lives, the lives of our children and of future generations, and even the survival of the planet are threatened. Despite being in the midst of material abundance and achievement, I am surrounded by anguished youth—some rushing blindly and heartlessly on their race to nowhere, others dropping out, numbed and disillusioned. My peace is shattered daily by the sharp blast of the train's whistle, reminding me daily of the five teens from my son's high school who took their own lives in a single year on the tracks near our home.

My sense of helplessness is a reflection of the vulnerability that many face in the world and provides a way of recognizing that our safety now depends on our loving and caring for the peoples of the world just as we love and care for our own families. Our survival depends on our willingness to transform ourselves into active global citizens. I see that my grandmother's teachings have meaning today in how to live a meaningful life, and I have been sharing them with people in many parts of the world.

I have put together some of Grandmother's teachings in this book, along with those of other mentors and guides. It is full of stories, as they make learning easier, and Grandmother loved telling them, as do I. My hope is that these stories will have meaning for you and help you to understand, and possibly even integrate, heartful principles into your life. Practice is necessary, so each chapter concludes with exercises that will help you to make the principles part of your daily activities.

Aging helps me overcome the fear that my words will not be listened to or will be misunderstood, and that what is most important to me must be made verbal and shared. I trust that a caring writer can bring new life to people by his honest self-portrait, as a service to those searching for some light in the midst of darkness. I believe that it is necessary for those of us who write, to live and speak the truths that we believe and know beyond understanding. We survive by taking part in a process of life that is creative and continuing.

I tell my story of learning from Grandmother's wisdom in the belief that what is most personal is most universal. Yet it's just our story, hers and mine, and I've chosen to live like this. It's my belief that everybody's life can be like this, if they too choose to make it so, to reflect about what they've been through, and to share that with others. I am tempted by the desire to appear wise but strive to tell only what I know—no more and no less.

The stories I tell in this book show how I am here today and who I have become because of the love of Grandmother and of others who have given their lives for me. Throughout my life I've been blessed with countless teachers, some of whom are honored here and others who remain nameless. My story is their story, as my life has relied on their love and guiding light.

The song "Ripple" ends with the words "If I knew the way, I would take you home"[1]—a reminder that we each must find our own way home. I am always on my way home. The path of heartfulness, though constantly challenging, has guided me, filling my life with wonder, truth, and beauty. I believe that it will also serve as a guide to finding *your* way home—transforming yourself and society with compassion, and making peace in yourself and in the world.

xxiii

INTRODUCTION

HEARTFULNESS

When we speak of mindfulness, it is important to keep in mind that we equally mean heartfulness. In fact, in Asian languages, the word for "mind" and the word for "heart" are usually the same. So if you are not hearing or feeling the word heartfulness when you encounter or use the word mindfulness, you are in all likelihood missing its essence.[1]

—JON KABAT-ZINN

Grandmother was proud of her ancestry and told me about the scroll with our genealogy written on it that was lost when our house was burned by fires from American bombs. The genealogy traced our family back to Michinaga Fujiwara, the most powerful man in Japan in the Heian period. Another of our ancestors was Saemon Matsumoto, the lord of a castle.

Grandmother grew up with my great-grandfather, one of the last samurai. She remembered him as a beautiful man—tall, long legs, fair-skinned, a long nose, and deep-set eyes—who people thought looked like a foreigner. I too am often seen as a foreigner, so was heartened when she claimed that I look a lot like him. She lauded the way he carried himself with dignity and without the immodesty of people who have money or power but no "decent family background." He was known as a kind, gentle, mild-mannered, true gentleman.

Great-grandfather was a quiet man, which was highly admired in those days, but Grandmother liked to stay by his side and ask him many questions.

Sometimes he would say, "Oh, it's not important, no need to talk about it." But at other times he told stories, such as how the family name was really Yamamoto, not Shigematsu. He had been a *hatamoto,* a high-ranking samurai, one of the Shogun's trusted warriors, a direct subject of Ieyasu Tokugawa. When the forces supporting the emperor rose up against them, there was a great battle in which both he and his brother were wounded. His brother survived a spear injury but later died of cholera. My great-grandfather was injured by a sword striking his wrist and was forced to flee. He made it to the sea by horse and then down the coast to where they bought a small fishing boat and with one hundred men set sail for the safe haven of friendly samurai. After several days they landed in a port on the island of Shikoku. When he got there, he changed the name to Shigematsu, to hide his identity.

She remembers watching him on days that he felt good and would sit in the garden. Holding his sword out in front of him, he would sprinkle it with flour and stare at the blade. Suddenly he would swipe at the air with a *whoosh!* He taught her that he lived by *Bushido,* the way of the warrior, that included contemplation of death in a daily ritual:

> Every morning and evening I calm my heart by contemplating death, considering myself as dead. Then I am able to live as though my body were already dead and am freed to live well.

Great-grandfather explained that he did not fear death and even wished for it. Yet he appreciated moments of beauty, when he could be filled with the wonder of nature and the fleeting cherry blossoms, feeling oneness with them in the impermanence of existence. In this way of living, with the awareness that, like the blossoms, we are all inevitably dying, lies a key to living fully in every breath, in every cup of tea.

Grandmother taught me that this is what is meant by the expression *Ichi-go, Ichi-e*—one moment, one meeting: a reminder to appreciate each moment as a once-in-a-lifetime opportunity. In daily life, this meant bearing all things in mind, not being distracted or forgetting what we are attending to. With these teachings, I felt myself coming alive in the spirit of *Bushido,* embracing death, living fully in each moment.

Grandmother loved teaching me life lessons with *kanji* characters that originated in China thousands of years ago. While the meaning of *kanji* has evolved over time and people today don't normally see deep meaning in deconstructing the *kanji,* to her they were rich with significance. I too became fascinated with them.

One that she taught me was the *kanji* for busy, 忙. It consists of two parts, one meaning heart and the other death. She said this means that we are not really living well if we are too preoccupied with thinking and doing, too busy to be present. "Busy" is when are minds are full, rather than mindful—times when we are not available for others. This reminds us that we are most alive when we are mindful, living fully in the present moment.

Grandmother surprised me by showing me another *kanji* composed similarly with the symbols for death and heart, 忘. This one signifies "to forget," which she said could have many meanings. The most basic is that we are spiritually dead when we forget who we are, with whom we are connected, who our ancestors are. It's a reminder that we are alive when we remember who we are and from where we come. The opposite of mindfulness is forgetfulness. We must remember that we are alive, as expressed in the *kanji* for one's nature, which combines heart and life, 性.

Grandmother said that the *kanji* for "forget" teaches us that we need to remember we are alive, to remember what we must do, and to live with our hearts. We need to remember the lessons we have learned, the teachings of our elders, and the times in life when we feel most alive. Remembering when we feel meaning, balance, connectedness, and wholeness will bring healing.

I saw that when I am moody and not fully alive, it is because I am living as if I were going to live forever, forgetting that I am in fact dying and will die. Remembrance of death helps me to come alive. *Bushido* taught me to incorporate the awareness of death into my daily living—not as a practice of thinking of my last hour, or of my physical death, but rather as always seeing life against the background of death. The challenge is to incorporate the awareness of dying into our every moment so as to become more fully alive. Death makes us warriors. Living with the awareness that death is near us makes us alert and alive.

Grandmother's stories helped me to remember how compassionate wisdom is passed on through stories. Spirituality, our connection to things beyond ourselves, is conveyed well by stories, which speak the language of the heart with words. Stories convey the mystery and the miracle, the adventure of being alive. They guide us to truth, knowledge, and beauty through words.

I remember many stories, and I will tell three here that especially enable me to develop heartfulness. These stories tell me who I am, with whom I am connected, and what I am called to do.

You Are Japanese

One unforgettable story I like to tell is of my adventure in summer camp when I was a boy. I thought camp would be endless fun. My two best friends, both older than me, were going, and I wanted to go with them so badly that I asked my dad to lie about my age so I could get in; I was seven and you were supposed to be at least eight. Dad liked my boldness so he agreed and I got to go to the two-week overnight camp.

Camp Russell wasn't quite what I had dreamed about. The Boy's Club camp was full of tough kids from all over the city. I heard them whispering to each other when I walked by, and soon little gangs were shouting, "Hey, Jap!" or "Ching, Chong, Chinaman!" Kids were laughing and mimicking Chinese. I was scared and didn't know what to do, so I acted like I didn't hear anything. No one approached me and

I heard them joking that they should beware because I knew karate. I didn't. But even though the kids didn't want to fight me I was still afraid the gangs would beat me. I was flooded with fear, terrified of the hatred in their faces and words.

While I avoided violence, my friends didn't. Joey was already shaving at 11 and when Shaun made fun of him for being so hairy Joey swung at him, forgetting that he still had a razor blade in his hand. Shaun screamed as blood spurted out of his neck and Joey started crying hysterically, apologizing like a madman. Both kids were sent home, leaving me alone. All my boldness in wanting to go to the camp for bigger kids was gone. This was my first time away from home, with no family or friends. I felt homesick, and at night in bed in the dark cabin I wished I was home with Mommy and Daddy and my big sisters.

After a week of camp my parents came to visit. I don't know how they got there because we didn't have a car. When they asked, "How's camp?" I lied and said, "It's okay." I wanted to be tough, but somehow I couldn't hide my pain any longer and started to whimper. I put my head down and began to sob, my little body shaking. I don't remember ever crying before that. My dad never cried and neither did I. As his only son, I knew he wanted me to be strong. I didn't want him to think I was a weak sissy. But he put his arm around me and held me to his big chest. So I let it all out.

I didn't explain much, just that kids were calling me names and my friends were gone. My dad said gently, "That's okay, you can come home. You don't have to stay." But as soon as he said that, I suddenly didn't feel like going home any more. After I calmed down and wiped my tears away, I told my parents I was staying. They lingered a little longer that afternoon, thinking I might change my mind, but when they saw that I was firm in my decision they went home without me, leaving me there for the final week.

The story speaks to me in many ways. I see it is as a story of trauma—a fire in which I was forged. I emerged scarred, forever vulnerable to being wounded and feeling victimized. It was a formative event in my relatively safe and secure life. It is also a story of vulnerability and courage. Wounded, I pulled myself back together with a resolution to be true to who I was. Somehow, even as a child I knew that this was the way to self-preservation and maintaining my dignity.

The story helps me to remember who I am. Being Japanese became crucially important to me early in life. This connection to a cultural heritage, a spiritual spring, was *heartfulness,* and I trusted it to carry me forward. I see how I had grown, as a result of my own courage and the help of others. I also realize how there are parts of us that have been pushed into the unconscious, where our childhood memories are kept. To me, healing is remembering and embracing those memories shrouded in darkness, thereby becoming more whole as they emerge into the light.

The Buddhist expression "Lion's Roar" came alive for me. I saw how, by connecting to our tender memories of vulnerability and feeling them fully, their energy becomes available to us. Overcoming terror of our own energy develops fearlessness toward the whole of life. The lion's roar is the brave assertion that anything, including our emotions, can be handled rather than taking us over.[2]

Heartfulness is based in the wisdom of diverse spiritual traditions. For me, it is important to connect with others who share the concern of integrating mindfulness with its spiritual roots in Zen. Some Zen practitioners criticize mindfulness as devoid of spirituality, while mindfulness practitioners criticize Zen as removed from reality of people's lives. The Zen 2.0 international conference in Kamakura, Japan, held in September 2017, brought together monks, mindfulness teachers, and concerned others to learn how we can connect and benefit from both Zen and mindfulness practice in the West.

Recent experiences I have had in many parts of Asia have made me acutely aware of the connection between mindfulness and culture. To make it more acceptable, mindfulness has been promoted in the West by disconnecting it from its diverse cultural roots. But for someone like myself, this removes it from a more genuine spiritual foundation. My Japanese cultural heritage is deeply connected to my understanding and practice of mindfulness. One can make sense of mindfulness by seeing how it is expressed in culture, philosophy, and language, and how it is integrated in daily life rituals and customs. Heartfulness is a way of making this connection central and crucial.

You Are Mixed

Another formative story I remember is from a scene in my childhood home, when my parents were engaging in a simple conversation at breakfast.

Mom began by saying, "The windows are dirty."

Dad glanced up from his newspaper and coffee and said, "Yeah."

Mom repeated, "They haven't been washed in a long time."

Dad mumbled, "Nope."

We kids went off to school; Mom went to work and Dad stayed home.

At dinner that night Mom was in a bad mood. Finally, Dad asked her, "What's wrong?"

Mom just said, "Nothing"

Dad persisted, "No, I can tell something's wrong"

Mom insisted, "Nothing"

But Dad knew it wasn't true, "Come on, Toshi, what's wrong?"

Mom finally relented, saying, "You know what's wrong"

"No, tell me."

"You didn't wash the windows."

"You didn't ask me to."

"Yes, I did"

"No, you didn't"

"Yes, I did"

"When?"

"This morning"

"What did you say?"

"I said, 'The windows are dirty.'"

"Oh, okay, but that's not the same as asking me to wash the windows."

"I even said, 'They haven't been washed for a long time.'"

"If you want me to wash the windows, you have to say it clearly, 'Please wash the windows.'"

Mom got in the final word, "Oh, why don't you listen! I said the windows are dirty. Why do I have to say, 'Wash the windows'? Anyone knows that's what you do when the windows are dirty."

Mom and Dad's struggle with communication symbolized the human need to express things in words, as well as the awareness of its futility. Their values about words were radically different. Mom was raised in a strict household where girls were expected to be silent. Children were schooled in the art of subtlety, indirectness, and allusions, learning to read cues and understand without being told. Words were viewed as often unnecessary and inadequate to express the finer human emotions. Her way of communicating was like that of the haiku poet Bashō, who said, "What's the point of saying everything with words?"

Dad was raised in the United States by Irish immigrant parents and believed that if you could just find the right words, you could say anything. He read voraciously and lived with a dictionary by his side, constantly looking up words as he read. He dramatically recited poetry. In his Judeo-Christian culture, words were sacred, as expressed in the Bible: "The word was God."

Perhaps my relating this story is a way of remembering that as a child I was immersed in two, sometimes dramatically different, cultures. Born as the child of a Japanese mother and an Irish-American father, I was enveloped in both cultures from the beginning. Mixture became a dominant theme in my life. I even pursued it as a career, becoming an early researcher in the area of mixed identities. It became natural for me to see things from this dual perspective. Whenever I was asked if I was Japanese or Irish, my obvious answer was that I was both. This answer did not always please others, as we like reality divided into neat and distinct parts, seeing it as one or the other: black or white, Japanese or Irish.

Early on, I saw intimately how there were ways of being, doing, thinking, and feeling that were equally real and neither right nor wrong. It was deeply ingrained in me that life was rarely an either/or situation but more like both/and. I experienced the mixed nature of the human condition in which we are able to aspire to be godlike and yet are humanly imperfect. I saw that we live in two realities, one offering glimpses into oneness and the other stuck in our own egos. To be human is to be fundamentally finite, to be essentially limited, and yet, at the same time, to be capable of wisdom and love that transcends limitations. I recognize that my family, my students, and even my country have no inherent reality. Yet I cannot deny that I remain deeply attached to all of them.

The practice of mindfulness brings me closer to the ancient wisdom of us humans as being essentially mixed, somehow in the middle. I bring learning from my mixed racial, national, and cultural experiences and identities to the teaching of heartfulness. Paradox and ambiguity reside at the heart of the human condition—our failures are our successes, our suffering is our joy, our imperfections prove to be the very source of our longing for perfection.

Mixed consciousness teaches us that only by embracing the dark side of our ambiguous natures can we ever come to know the light.

You Care

A third heartful story that I remember comes from my days at Harvard University when I was a student training to be a clinical psychologist. A group of us were hired by the school system in Savannah, Georgia, to randomly test that city's children. We learned later that the superintendent of schools wanted to prove that the children, mostly African-American, were of average intelligence, and therefore capable of performing well in school. He hoped that this would motivate the mostly white teachers to raise their standards, their expectations, and the performance of the children. An article in the Savannah newspaper some months later declared: "Harvard shows Savannah children of average IQ."

I was administering an IQ test one day to a 12-year-old boy named

Jerome. We were in the Vocabulary section. The word was *justice.* Jerome didn't answer so I repeated: *"justice."* A smirk came on his face but he still didn't answer, so I gave him a third chance: "What's *justice* mean, Jerome?" As I was about to move on to the next item, he blurted out, "Can't get none of it!"

His answer stunned me. I looked at him, he smiled mischievously, and I moved on to the next item to cover my discomfort.

Later that evening when I was scoring his test, I saw that the scoring guideline did not contain the example "Can't get none of it." It wasn't a two-point answer, it wasn't a one-point answer, so it was a zero-point answer. Jerome would get zero for a question to which he obviously knew the answer. I asked myself, Where is the justice in this system? Who makes the questions and answers? Whose children score well on this test? Who doesn't score well and gets placed in special education or simply labeled as unintelligent? Who had ever seen the intelligence in Jerome?

By retelling this story, I remember how much I have been enlivened by the realities of diversity and social justice. Heartfulness for me involves a concern for those left out, the marginalized, those denied equal rights and fair treatment. My public emergence in the field of mindfulness relatively late in my career has required overcoming the barrier to what I perceived as an exclusive space of color blindness. Now I see more self-reflection on how the belief of having transcended certain worldly concerns leads to dismissing issues of dire importance for some people. I am heartened by a movement for mindfulness spaces to be more inclusive, and am connecting with others who are actively asserting themselves.

I encounter people who are realizing that while things like race don't matter in the sense of their ultimate meaning, they *do* matter a great deal in the daily lives of many people. They may even be life-or-death issues. Heartfulness is a way to deepen awareness and understanding of human diversity. Those whose personal and professional lives have focused on this can play a role in encouraging mindfulness communities to embrace diversity and to promote inclusion.

A popular image of mindfulness is that it means being self-centered, yet we can better reframe our inner work as a collective, communal, and connected way of being. In the movement from "me" to "we," our concern for others develops into wider and wider circles of inclusion. The personal growth promoted by mindfulness can, however, be stymied unless space and place are provided for further development. The work of transforming society begins by transforming ourselves, by making peace *in* ourselves. A heartful vision and practice of living extends to compassion by focusing on our interconnectedness, by uniting compassion with responsibility, and by acting to relieve suffering in the world.

The three stories just told are real medicine, reminding me who I am, what I believe, and what I live for. The first story forged the development of an identity that found fulfillment in a homecoming journey to discover my roots. Returning to Japan to live connected me to a spiritual source. The second story formed the foundation of an academic career in which I studied mixed identities that connected me to the truth of our dual realities of perfection and imperfection. And the third story nourished my lifelong activism in issues of social justice and diversity, connecting me to the expression of love in action. I saw the truths from these and other stories and realized that they could help others, who of course also have their own stories to tell. From the three stories I derived basic elements of heartfulness to be mindfulness, compassion, and responsibility. I saw eight ways of cultivating heartfulness: beginner's mind, vulnerability, authenticity, connectedness, listening, acceptance, gratitude, and responsibility.

Why Heartfulness?

Heartfulness describes a way of being in mindfulness, in compassion, and in responsibility. The word *mindfulness,* by itself, seems insufficient to explain how mindful consciousness extends into compassion and is expressed in active caring. Heartfulness portrays this expansive sense of living with openness and clarity, being true to ourselves, acting in sympathy with all beings, resonating with and being part of the world around us. The word *com-passion* literally means "feeling with," and is enabled by first being willing to feel what you feel, opening up a certain rawness and tenderness.

Today's mindfulness movement is full of potential. Mindfulness training programs in diverse settings, including schools, businesses, and governmental agencies, offer good training in reducing stress and increasing the powers and flexibility of ordinary mental processes. Making mindfulness more of a biological, cognitive, brain activity has helped many people overcome resistance to it, as evidence-based research findings convince many that it is legitimate.

However, the focus on science also takes mindfulness further from the heart by making it an activity that can be done pragmatically for its benefits. This perpetuates the illusion that we can achieve anything through our intellect and willpower. The science focus disguises the reality that truth, beauty, and kindness are not reached merely by rationally and logically thinking our way to them.

Our love of technology and faith in science is countered by the recognition that these will never provide what we need to live with meaning. We realize that no matter how advanced we become, regardless of how sophisticated our gadgets are and how many of them we possess, they will not give us the essential elements of a good life. A meaningful life is focused in the heart and filled with compassion and giving.

Heartfulness seeks to overcome limitations to the kind of mindfulness that is used for the pursuit of profit and pleasure and doesn't challenge materialistic beliefs, values, or practices.[3] Mindfulness can enable other virtues, but if we remain on the purely cognitive level, or stay narrowly focused on stress reduction, we are missing its true power. While the science focus is extremely convincing as to the reality of the power of mindful practice, we also need to maintain and expand the heart's role in mindfulness.

Mindfulness is still becoming equated with the individual pursuit of happiness, with people seeking pleasure and more joy, with less stress and less involvement. Yet the popular culture's adoption of mindfulness risks losing its original meaning. Heartfulness emphasizes purpose through connecting to something larger than the individual self. A heartful life finds meaning in making a difference in the lives of others.

A beautiful expression of this evolving form of mindfulness is in the Japanese word *kokoro* 心. While minds and hearts are separated in a Western sense, with mind referring to thinking capacity and heart meaning emotions and sentimental feelings, in Eastern thought they are the same reality. In Asia, people often point to their chest when referring to mind as an openness or a wakefulness that resonates with the world around them, rather than something created or possessed by their own brain or ego.

The word *heartfulness* brings us closer to the meaning of *kokoro* and the deep meaning of mindfulness. *Kokoro* unites feeling, emotion, mind, and spirit—the whole person—and seems close to the word *heartfulness.* This word appears in Jon Kabat-Zinn's writings since the 1990s, in which he suggests that another way to think of the gentle, appreciative, and nurturing way of mindfulness is to use the word *heartfulness.*[4] He later warns that many people are not equating mindfulness with the heart, thereby missing its true essence. Heartfulness is opening and cultivating the heart through inner stillness and silence, becoming more human, more compassionate, and more responsible, both to one's own self and to all other beings.

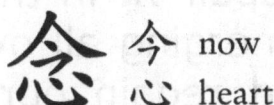

Heartfulness

The meaning of heartfulness is expressed in the *kanji* 念. It consists of two parts, the top part 今, meaning "now"; the bottom part ♥, meaning "heart." This symbol clearly expresses the sense of being wholly present in the moment. Living in a state of heartfulness means listening to one's heart, to one's inner voice, affecting our relationship with ourselves as well as our relationships with our family, with our work, and with the larger world.

Heartful Community

> I believe that we are at the point now in the United States where a movement is beginning to emerge ... demanding that instead of just complaining about these things, or just protesting about these things, we begin to look for, and hope for, another way of living.... I see hope beginning to trump despair ... in the many small groups emerging all over the place, to try and regain our humanity in very practical ways.[5]
> —GRACE LEE BOGGS

Like the individual psychotherapy that I practice, mindfulness is a solitary activity. But heartfulness is practiced in groups with the clear goal of creating community, a sense of openness, direct communion with others, and an awareness of oneself as part of something greater. Grounding our encounters in mindfulness enables vulnerability and authenticity. People realize connectedness, engage in deep listening, feel more accepting, and are grateful for what is happening. Mindfulness is a path, not an ending—something to be practiced, put into action. It fosters the awareness of being connected to the self, to something beyond the self, and indeed to everything and everyone.

In my work as a psychotherapist and teacher, I know that while some learning takes place in isolation, it can be greatly intensified and accelerated in the company of others, where we can put what we are learning into practice—mindfulness in action. In much of the world, healing is a process done in community, characterized by synergy, in which therapeutic power is unlimited, expandable, and possessed and shared by all. The process of heartfulness focuses on groups as entities in which healing and learning the art of living with others can be done.

The work of heartfulness consists of bringing people together in classes or workshops and developing inclusive communities. Research and experience tell us that intimate contact between people of diverse backgrounds can reduce prejudice if we share common goals, show a sense of cooperation, and have equal status.[6] Pushing back the tables, sitting in a circle, we demonstrate the transformation of consciousness that often occurs during simple, everyday exchanges, when all present are treated with respect. We listen carefully to each other and acknowledge the speaker by saying, "We see you; we hear you." Even engaging in mundane concerns touches our spirit and enhances consciousness in ways that do not need to be radical or intense; often, learning consists merely of a subtle shift in perspective.

In these groups we open ourselves up to ways of knowing beyond scientific rationalism. We understand through experience rather than using intellectual reasoning to reach a logical conclusion. We affirm the unity of mind and body and of the spiritual with the material. We believe that we are not victims limited to and bound by the past. Crossing boundaries brings joy. Rather than seeking the answers, we try to live the questions—now.

We consciously strive to create "heartful community," based on the mutual understanding and respect that result from sharing voices and storytelling. Our sense of cooperation is enhanced by the values we practice—beginner's mind, vulnerability, authenticity, connectedness, acceptance, listening, gratitude, and service. Together, we learn through nurturing and caring in relationships with others.

Our purpose is to cross borders within ourselves as well as between us and others, so that we can cultivate the ability to see the positive even in apparently opposing worldviews, trying to understand and empathize. We value well-being that involves multiple forms of self-care and compassion for others, healing by connecting to all parts of our self and others.

Heartful communities are grounded in storytelling. We expand the boundaries of our stories, allowing room for narratives of difference, seeking more compassionate ways of relating to one another. No one's stories are privileged; we listen and try to understand where others' stories come from and how are they situated within our various embodied experiences of the world.

Heartfulness provides for our needs in finding identity, meaning, and purpose in life through connections to the community, to the natural world, and to spiritual values. We are integrating the inner and outer life, actualizing a sense of individual and global responsibility. In our communities, we are acknowledging and embracing our humanness alongside our aspiration to go beyond ourselves, bringing these two together synergistically. We connect more with the heart, extending the circles of compassion more widely to include responsibility to others.

Eight Ways of Cultivating Heartfulness

This book is organized around a way of being and living that is called heartfulness. In my grandmother's teachings and in my life stories I identify eight principles for cultivating heartful living. These are learned from observing life circumstances, engaging in self-reflection, studying human nature, practicing mindfulness, counseling, teaching, parenting, and partnering. There is considerable overlap in the principles, which form the core of the chapters in this book, and there is nothing sacred about the number; they are only the ones that I have identified:

Beginner's Mind
Vulnerability
Authenticity
Connectedness
Listening
Acceptance
Gratitude
Service

EXERCISES

I. Mindfulness Meditation

This is a meditation on experiencing mindfulness.

1. Sit quietly in a chair with both feet on the ground and your hands in your lap.
2. Close your eyes and bring your attention to your breathing. Notice the breath as it enters your body through your nose and travels to your lungs. Feel how the inward breaths are cool and outward breaths are warm, and notice where the breath travels as you inhale and exhale.
3. Just observe your thoughts, don't fight them, and gently bring your awareness back to your breath.
4. Do this exercise for 5 minutes daily for one week, lengthening the time by a few minutes each day.

There are many resources online that will give you more detailed instructions and guidelines. Here's one:

www.mindful.org/mindfulness-how-to-do-it/

II. Loving-Kindness Meditation

This is a meditation on showing loving-kindness to self and others.

1. Follow the directions in exercise I for meditation. Then focus attention on your heart center. You may want to place one or both of your hands over your heart center.
2. Say these words to yourself:
   May I be well
   May I be happy
   May I be peaceful
   May I be loved

3. Bring your attention back to your heart center and feel the warmth there.
4. Next, bring to mind the image of someone you love—a person or a pet, either living or deceased.
5. Say these words to the loved one:
   May you be well
   May you be happy

May you be peaceful
May you be loved

6. Bring your attention to your heart center and feel the warmth there. Visualize loving-kindness spread throughout your body. Feel it move out of your body to touch the loved one.
7. This meditation can continue by extending loving-kindness to many different people—someone who is sick or suffering; someone whom you feel indifferent about; someone with whom you are having difficulties.

Many resources are available online on the loving-kindness meditation. Here's one:

   ggia.berkeley.edu/practice/loving_kindness_meditation

1

BEGINNER'S MIND

If your mind is empty, it is always ready for anything; it is open to everything. In the beginner's mind there are many possibilities; in the expert's mind there are few.... When we have no thought of achievement, no thought of self, we are true beginners. Then we can really learn something. The beginner's mind is the mind of compassion. When our mind is compassionate, it is boundless.... Then we are always true to ourselves, in sympathy with all beings, and can actually practice.[1]
—SHUNRYU SUZUKI

Fresh out of college, without a job, and needing some money to pay the rent, I reluctantly became a substitute teacher in the Cambridge, Massachusetts, public schools. Substitute teaching in inner city public schools in the United States was a taxing job, with the goal of simply surviving to the end of the day. The tough city kids were too much for me. They ate me up from the ring of the opening bell and spit me out when it mercifully rang after last period, signaling that the punishment was over. I was desperate for anything that would help me to do more than just make it through the day, and one morning while walking to a new school I got a brilliant idea.

I strode confidently into my fifth-grade classroom, though only a few kids seemed to notice or care. I faced them, told them to sit down and be quiet—in Japanese. They all turned and stared at me. I repeated my directions. Their incredulous looks turned to smiles. They peppered me with questions:

"What did you say?"

"You okay, mister?"

"What language you speaking?"

I looked at them, feigning disbelief.

"I'm speaking Japanese. Don't you understand?"

They shouted back, "No, man; teach us Japanese!"

And so I did, and the day flew by. I taught them how to say "hello" and how to write their names. I had their interest and attention. They were curious and eager learners. And they were fresh, all beginners with many possibilities.

I got a steady job shortly after that and forgot about that glorious day. But a few years later as I was walking through that same part of the city I heard someone call out, "Hey, mister!"

I turned and faced a smiling young teenager.

"You're the guy who taught us Japanese!"

I suddenly realized that it was Ricardo, now an adolescent, the student who had been most excited and enthusiastic about learning Japanese from me years earlier. I recalled the note the teacher had left for me warning that Ricardo was one of the kids who would be "oppositional" and "hostile" to learning. But with me he had had a fresh start and was simply being there—attentive, aware, awake, and appreciative. He could leave the past behind and not worry about the future. For me, it was an indelible and unforgettable experience in understanding how we learn and how we teach.

I understood Ricardo's experience through Zen. He had "beginner's mind"; he was on fire. The sky was the limit. He was not held back by others' perceptions of who he was and what he could or could not do. There were infinite possibilities. He was *mindful*.

My experience in schools was different. I was rewarded by teachers and felt great pressure always to score high on tests and maintain top grades—that was more important than learning. School was oppressive, heavy, memorizing facts for tests, and listening to lessons that were not taught in a way that was fun and exciting. I rarely experienced the joy of learning that Ricardo must have felt when learning basic Japanese.

I had learned about beginner's mind at home. My mother was always reminding me to wake up, focus, stop dreaming, pay attention, not be forgetful, and do what needed to be done, *now.* My storyteller father's way of teaching was different, calling on me to pay attention to the wonder and mystery of life, to joy and sorrow, demanding full engagement with human encounters. He was forever childlike, always asking his kids to look at something with a beginner's mind, with feelings of curiosity, levity, and fascination. He embodied joie de vivre, proclaiming Albert Einstein's view that one could live as if nothing was a miracle, or as if *everything* was a miracle.

But out in the world, when I acted mindfully by being patient, silent, listening, and being nonjudgmental, I was regarded as strange. I was often teased for being mindful, for example, reflecting on another's view rather than asserting a strong opinion of my own, and even for being a slow, conscientious eater. It seemed that other kids were already moving on to the next thing while I was still sniffing the flowers, rolling around with the dogs, or wanting to play baseball even when it became too dark to see. A high school teacher who noticed the joy with which I experienced being one with the natural world had nicknamed me "Nature Boy."

I realized that American society regards being mindful as weird and even laughable, while rushing around busily with a mind full of thoughts is considered normal. People found it strange that I reveled in the beauty of whatever was transpiring in the moment.

As I grew up I saw that public displays of beginner's mind and mindful living could draw unwanted attention from the wrong people. One warm, sunny spring day when I was a college student and the cherry trees were in full bloom, I was rushing through Harvard Yard on my way to class. I suddenly paused to appreciate a beautiful pink cloud, reminding myself to be mindful. I stopped by a tree, closed my eyes, and took a deep breath. The delicate fragrance of the blossoms was intoxicating. I focused my attention on my breath and being in the moment. I took another breath. I must have taken a few more because I was suddenly startled by a voice.

"What are you doing?"

I opened my eyes and turned around to find a policeman eyeing me suspiciously.

"What are you doing?" he repeated.

I was completely caught off guard and felt unsure how to explain what I was doing.

"Nothing," was all I could say.

"Are you on drugs?" he asked.

I wanted to say, "No sir, I don't need drugs, I am high on just being mindful—fully present, aware, awake, appreciative"—but I didn't. I just mumbled, "No," and walked away.

Mindfulness brings tension, as it is out of tune with the dominant current of busyness, putting you out of sync with all those people rushing madly through life or tuning out. Throughout my youth, people found my patience annoying; my silence made them anxious. They wanted me to talk more, and often asked: "Why don't you raise your hand?" "Why are you so quiet, so shy, so reserved, so slow, so accepting?" "Why aren't you more brash, outspoken, argumentative, quicker, more demanding?" These societal and cultural pressures confused me at a time and in a place where mindfulness was unappreciated. I may have been naturally mindful, but I came to disrespect it in a world in which it's considered better to be constantly busy.

Ichi-go, Ichi-e

Remembering Ricardo's story renews my appreciation for the richness and freshness of living with beginner's mind. I recall the many ways I have found of exploring mindfulness—including yoga, meditation, aikido, macrobiotics, qi gong. I even took up the study of East Asian medicine with a feeling of wonder and awe.

My grandmother's teaching about *Ichi-go, Ichi-e*—cherishing each moment—held special meaning. I sought to bring full awareness to the life-and-death struggle of every human encounter, treasuring meetings with people as one chance in my lifetime that will never happen again. Though at first I had a hard time appreciating the tea ceremony, it was where I experienced *Ichi-go, Ichi-e* most strongly. Seeing the host conducting the ritual with true sincerity, taking care and devoting herself entirely to every detail, instilled awareness and presence in me. When offered a cup of tea, to truly appreciate it, I needed to be mindful, concentrating on it, so that it could reveal its fragrance and taste to me.

Applying this to daily life, *Ichi-go, Ichi-e* told me that all we have is the present moment. We should not miss the opportunity that is given to us now. If we can consider the reality that every encounter is one of a kind, and therefore something to be treasured as if it is the one time in our life, we will value the time. Approaching life in this way, we will have an abundance of enriched moments.

Immersion in Japanese culture renewed my respect for mindfulness as a way in which I could be truly alive by continually touching life deeply in every moment, even in the most mundane of activities. I sensed that life is in the here-and-now, that we can discover peace within ourselves simply by being aware of our breath, by realizing the miracle of being alive. While mindfulness is rooted in meditation, it can be practiced in our ordinary daily activities: making a little time in our life for being still, not doing anything, and tuning in to our breathing. Every moment is an opportunity for practice and development. In this way we cultivate appreciation for the richness of each moment we are alive.

The experience with Ricardo awakened me, at the time, to the possibilities in education if we could be fully present and attentive, though this transformative event was forgotten and lay dormant for years. It was years later that I remembered, when I was first asked to lecture at the Stanford University School of Medicine. As I pondered how to instill the most important lessons of culture and medicine in my listeners, I recalled that amazing experience. It had worked then with fourth graders, so I decided to give it a try.

To my delight, I found that it was as effective with medical students as it had been with children. This time I followed the mini-performance by explaining that I was disrupting their expectations as a way of bringing their attention to the present moment. I assured them that I was "mindful" and hoped that they, too, would be as fully present in the moment as they could be. This experience was a way of reminding them to be mindful in their work as future health professionals—attentive, listening, seeing the uniqueness in each patient.

I was presenting them with a "disorienting dilemma," an experience that does not fit their expectations and forces them to consider new possibilities as they attempt to make sense of what is happening. This creates openness to learning by challenging assumptions of what is supposed to happen.

My brief performance of speaking Japanese, in other settings, has become a useful way of inducing mindfulness, drawing students and listeners into the moment by experiencing rather than being told. By presenting myself in a performative, playful way, I invite students to bring themselves fully into the classroom, with attention to what is happening in the moment, with awareness, acceptance, and appreciation. And the attention they give to me will then be extended to themselves and to their classmates.

Speaking to students in a language foreign to them is a way of inducing vulnerability—a key to education—as a lifelong commitment to self-reflection rather than as a detached mastery of a finite body of knowledge. Vulnerability means appreciating mystery as much as mastery; being comfortable with not-knowing, ambiguity, uncertainty, and complexity; cultivating awe and wonder that deepens our knowledge.

This is the lightness of beginner's mind, rather than the heaviness of needing to be competent. Feelings of vulnerability may be unsettling, but they are a way of understanding the importance of balancing a sense of competence with humility, remaining open to complexity despite our desire for simplicity.

Beginning encounters with this type of exercise enhances the sense of *Ichi-go, Ichi-e,* as students at every level come to regard each class as a once-in-a-lifetime opportunity. Research shows that students become more focused, more self-aware, and more aware of and less judgmental of self and others.[2] This creates greater opportunities for learning from the teacher as well as from fellow students.

As a teacher, from preschool to medical school, I've seen how attention is essential for learning, and so I continually integrate mindful practices in my teaching to achieve presence.

Focusing our attention connects us to our inner knowledge—what we already know—and brings it forth so that we can engage in new learning. This knowledge of seeing and thinking with the heart might be called presencing[3] or emotional intelligence.[4] Being mindfully in tune with this knowledge leads to positive, affirming acts, saying "yes" to the present moment, saying "yes" to life.

The Heart of Education

While I find great wisdom in *kanji*, I also discover deep meaning in the Latin origin of words. The Latin origin of "education," *educere,* means to lead forth. This spoke to me as a high school student disillusioned by education as practiced in American schools. As a young man, I hungered to move beyond traditional learning that values rational knowledge, scientific methods, and information about that which is outside us. Now I seek to respond to the desire to integrate learning with our lives, by enhancing wisdom that comes from self-reflection and expressing it in actions for self-care and compassion for others.

A heartful approach calls on students to actively situate themselves within the content of what they study, deepening their understanding of the material by discovering it in themselves, and then applying the concepts learned to their own lives. Our focus on compassion and connection to others satisfies the desire for inquiry into the nature of their minds through personal meaning, creativity, and insight, providing guidance in living a more spiritual life.

Heartfulness is guided by feminist scholar bell hooks' view of education as "an act of love ... as something that promotes our spiritual and mental growth."[5] Studying things in this way brings refreshing forms of knowing that go beyond the knowledge that values rationality, detached objectivity, and facts that we can't actually apply to our lives. Students continually remind me that mindful inquiry and the development of awareness is not a purely intellectual or cognitive process but part of a person's total way of living their life.[6]

Similarly for the physicist Arthur Zajonc, the true heart of education consists of loving what we study, as we come to know best that which we love the most. "We pause to reflect before speaking, quietly engage the issue inwardly before acting, open ourselves to not-knowing before certainty arises, and so we live for a time in the question before the answer emerges.... Only under such conditions can imagination work.... Poetry, indeed all art as well as science, flows from such restraint."[7]

This kind of education can be practiced at every level of school. More and more educators are integrating various mindfulness practices into their classrooms to help students focus and calm themselves, cultivate greater emotional intelligence, and develop their creativity. These practices enable deep introspection into meaning, ethics, purpose, and values, encouraging students' reflection on their internal experience as well as their connectedness with others.[8]

A number of studies of programs that directly train students in mindfulness have collectively demonstrated a range of cognitive, social, and psychological benefits to elementary, middle, and high school students. This research shows positive effects in many areas related to learning, including attention and focus, as well as creativity, memory, and cognitive capacities like retention and autonomous learning.[9]

School programs that focus on achieving benefits of behavioral control and cognitive focus often stop there; a heartful approach, by contrast, extends mindfulness to include benefits of increased compassion and responsibility. Research shows that mindfulness is correlated not only with focus on self and subject matter, but also with focus on others.[10] It seems to enhance flexible thinking, openness to novelty, alertness to distinction, sensitivity to different contexts, and implicit awareness of multiple perspectives—all qualities essential for developing diversity and inclusion. Mindfulness also enhances social skills by improving our ability to realize our deep connectedness with others through empathy and kindness. Useful in maintaining classroom control, it has far greater benefits for the learning and well-being of students.

Beginner's Mind in Health Care

My experience in education ranges from caring for 18-montholds in day care to adult learning. I teach in medical schools because I have also had a career as a clinical psychologist, training and working in hospitals, clinics, and schools. These experiences have nurtured my appreciation for the role of mindfulness in health care. One formative experience I had was with East Asian medicine. Having given up on Western medicine, I underwent acupuncture treatment for nagging headaches and failing vision that had occurred from a traumatic injury. A few months later, the pain was reduced and I threw away my eyeglasses. I also received treatments for a gastrointestinal disorder and vowed to become a practitioner of East Asian medicine, abandoning the mainstream path to becoming a doctor.

Returning to Japan, I apprenticed to a master named Tsutomu Tokuda, exchanging English lessons for his teaching of acupuncture, moxibustion, and shiatsu massage. Dr. Tokuda was blind and yet possessed great sensitivity to the body in ways that I did not. He often berated me for not being mindful, pointing out how my mind lacked focused attention and therefore could not detect the subtleties in pulse diagnosis or other ways of sensing disturbance in organs. He also strongly encouraged me to study mainstream medicine to complement what I was learning from him, pointing out bitterly how he was limited by his blindness, while I was not.

Another mentor, Hidehiko Mitsufuji, director of the largest East Asian medical center in Japan, was an M.D. who helped me to see the power in gaining mainstream medical training. So I went back to my original path, returning to the United States for medical school. However, once the path was opened I had the striking realization that it was not my way, as I did not naturally think in a reductionist, scientific way. I see things more holistically, what the writer and scientist Goethe described as "gentle empiricism," a way of scientific inquiry in which we approach the object of our attention without distorting it, by being gentle, listening, feeling—becoming one with the object of study.[11]

Now without a clear path, I wandered the streets of Cambridge, where I was living at the time, and came across a sign for the Harvard University School of Education. I walked in without thinking and was told that they had the right program for me and even the teachers I needed. In the next few weeks I met three—Richard Katz, Chester Pierce, and Kiyo Morimoto—and had the wonderful experience of being both seen and heard. In an incredible and unimaginable turn of events, I soon became a student at Harvard.

The program was based in clinical psychology but at heart was an innovative, interdisciplinary program that encompassed a wider vision of public practice and organizational consulting. Katz brought his unique background in cultural anthropology and studies of illness and healing that fit well with my experience in East Asian medicine. Pierce was a psychiatrist who taught cross-racial counseling, what I imagined would be my area of specialization. Their work had a tremendous influence on me, as you will see.

Morimoto offered a blend of humanistic psychology with Japanese culture that seemed natural to me and with which I deeply resonated. He taught the importance of heartfulness in counseling, the healing power of presence. Mori moto continually urged us students to not distance ourselves emotionally because of the difficulty of sitting with someone else's pain. He implored us to not abandon our clients, trusting that even when we think we have nothing more to offer we can always provide human company.

With Morimoto's guidance, I learned to trust my intuition that I could offer something valuable simply by *being there*. I realized that mindfulness was as important in counseling as it was in acupuncture, and it became the foundation of my therapy practice. This truth was most apparent in my training as a hospice counselor; at the bedside of a dying person, when I despaired that I had nothing to offer, we simply breathed together.

Mindfulness became integrated into my work in counseling in diverse cultural contexts as the enabler of deeper self-understanding and better understanding of others. When I am as fully present as possible, this allows the other person to bring himself or herself as completely as possible to the encounter. Listening, seeing, witnessing the wound, pain, or trauma, become the source of healing.

I remembered that I have always valued being there for someone; listening was something I offered others. In deep listening, I became one with the talker. For me, setting limits was the problem: knowing where, when, and how to stop. Learning self-care, understanding responsibility, and comprehending my unique purpose were important, developmentally. Gaining training and much practice as a counselor provided the concept of professional distance that I (somewhat reluctantly) learned to apply pragmatically to human relations in general.

Reflecting on my experiences in health care, I see using beginner's mind as bringing one into a state of mindfulness that is crucial in healing. This is true for both doctor and patient. Different modalities of healing provide various ways of relieving disturbing symptoms and each may claim to treat only a limited range of symptoms. But relieving those places of distress may open the person to the possibilities of greater changes. But whatever modality is used, there is always something about efficacy that cannot be explained by science, forcing us to acknowledge the elusive healing element of the heart.

My teachers in East Asian medicine acknowledged that the psychological and spiritual elements were important to consider, but were not directly addressed by their treatments. Still, Dr. Tokuda described his art as healing energy, or *Ki,* coming through him into the needle inserted into the patient's body at an acupuncture point. His awareness that his physiological intervention was also treating the person's spirit demonstrates heartfulness.

The counseling and hospice care that I learned in my training consciously called for beginner's mind and mindfulness. We students were asked to come to each encounter with fresh eyes and with the clear goal of simply being present. The possibility of our being open and vulnerable then appeared, calling forth our deepest human response to the other person. Heartfulness occurs when we enter into this space.

Mindfulness Based Stress Reduction has popularized this form of clinical care in hospitals globally. The results are being impressively documented in research.[12] While the focus of this practice is stress reduction, it can also potentially lead to compassion for others. The benefits can extend far beyond the individual's symptom relief to responsible action that brings meaning and purpose to living.

Heartfulness starts with beginner's mind and mindfulness, with the possibility of moving far beyond the personal health benefits. Beginner's mind is characterized by curiosity, a word that shares the same root as *cure.* This suggests that when we give our attention to what we love we can be drawn toward compassionate healing.[13]

Parenting

Before you cross the street
Take my hand

> Life is what happens to you
> While you're busy making other plans[14]

In John Lennon's song "Beautiful Boy," we see a mundane example of heartful parenting, helping a child to live in the moment rather than in the future. Sometimes it's the other way around, as children are by nature more mindful than adults. In heartful parenting we are open to learning from our children, as they call us to cultivate the capacity for openhearted, present-moment awareness. We practice heartful parenting when we are attending as fully as possible to each moment, seeing our children clearly, as they *are,* not as we wish to see them from our expectations, fears, and needs.[15]

My extensive training in psychology, medicine, and education helped prepare me for my greatest challenge as a parent. For 27 years I have found parenting to be a demanding way of cultivating heartfulness as a way of life, for it requires full presence in responding compassionately to the moment-to-moment demands of caring for another's needs. Feeding my children, changing their diapers, bathing them, cleaning up their mess, getting them off to school, taking them shopping, playing with them, cooking for them—everything became part of my practice of heartfulness.

If I can truly see and listen to my children, I am more able to be openhearted and nonjudgmental. I am more aware of what's happening in their lives and better able to know what I, their parent, need to do in each situation. I hope for greater wisdom to lead my children to live with purpose and meaning, neither neglecting them nor focusing narrowly only on their achievements and certain desired forms of future success.

The words of the poet Kahlil Gibran speak to me: *"You are the bows from which your children as living arrows are sent forth."*[16]

Heartful parenting means respecting the deep connection between us as parents and our children. They can even be our teachers, as they may question everything we know, providing endless opportunities for being mindful. Their challenging gives us many occasions to practice patience, clarity, and emotional balance.

We can learn the essence of heartful parenting from other parents whose children have terminal illnesses and short life expectancies. For some parents, it's painfully obvious that the end will come early. Their experiences teach them how to parent for the here-and-now, for the sake of parenting, for the humanity implicit in the act itself, cherishing every last moment together.

Heartful parenting reminds us that living for the future is an illusion. Some parents attempt to raise children who outpace all their peers, who achieve status, security, and safety. But heartful parenting means loving our children today, being authentic, respecting our children and ourselves as best we can. A friend of mine, Hatsuko Arima, who lost her child to cancer, reminds me to keep trying to discover a way of parenting that leads to deep connection and love both for my children and for myself.

Hatsuko is the mother of twins born with cystic fibrosis. When her daughter Ana passed away in 2013 after an incredible journey of 41 years surviving cystic fibrosis and two double-lung transplants, Hatsuko received many sympathetic condolences. But she confessed that while sadness was certainly there, she was also filled with joy from deep gratitude that Ana had received 41 years of life and was able to accomplish so much. From Ana's birth she had been prepared to expect a short life for her child. Parenting with a consciousness that time is limited for one's child can give appreciation for the preciousness of each day.

Heartful parenting may involve no more, and no less, than respecting and listening to your child. Those of us whose children do not have terminal illnesses live with the belief that our children have a future for which we must prepare them. But the reality is that this is not necessarily true. Some of our children are taken from us long before we have planned. And for those who are not, parenting our children for the future may rob us of the mindful presence required to see and listen to them in a way that enables us to respond to them in the present moment.

Heartful parenting means having moment-to-moment awareness and appreciation of daily blessings, balancing the need to prepare our children for a future while reminding ourselves to never neglect living fully—and to love them each day.

Beginner's Mind in Leadership

At exactly eight o'clock in the morning, the commanding officer announced, "Let's get started!" I nodded and said, "Yes, thank you, let's begin, and let's start by looking at what's happening here. Who's leading this session?" The room was quiet and everyone was listening intently. "I'm the designated leader of this session," I asserted, and several people nodded. Then I asked, "Who's telling us it's time to start?" Smiles appeared on their faces, and even the officer sensed where we were going. With a sense of beginner's mind, we began to explore what this simple interaction meant for the officer's style of leadership, his way of taking charge of situations, and how it affected those who worked for him. The room was filled with subordinates on his team, and we reflected on micro-managing, delegating authority, mentoring, and the underlying issues of trust, responsibility, and accountability. This was the beginning of a heartfulness leadership workshop I conducted for the U.S. Navy.

The members of that workshop focused on exploring their inner lives, their ways of being in the world, and their expression in how they would lead others. The commanding officer admitted to being ambivalent about mindfulness, fearing that it meant sitting around doing nothing while someone else was getting ahead by *doing*. He worried that if he became more present and calm, he would be regarded as spacey, impractical, and passive and would lose his competitive edge and so be unable to deal with important problems that occurred. He needed to be convinced that he would actually be more alert, be more efficient, and have greater well-being.

Together, we reflected on how leadership demands more than simply controlling. It includes personal competencies of self-awareness, self-regulation, and motivation. Leaders need emotional intelligence, including social competencies like empathy and the ability to induce desirable responses in others, influencing them to perform at their peak.[17] Heartfulness is a way of cultivating emotional intelligence, with the result that we become more aware of our feelings and better able to control them. It also enhances our social awareness and relationship management by making us more conscious of our position as team leader.

We viewed leadership through the lens of VUCA, a military concept that strategy must now be based on a world that is Volatile, Uncertain, Complex, and Ambiguous. This calls for a leader to have a new VUCA based in Vulnerability, Understanding, Connectedness, and Agility. Vulnerability is expressed as openness and humility; Understanding self and others is crucial; leaders must actively Connect with others: and they must be flexible and Agile.[18]

In our workshop, we were developing these leadership competencies in a safe and supportive environment where leaders risk vulnerability, examining their strengths and the areas in which they need to improve. We can all be more heartful leaders by learning how to monitor and adapt our emotions and behaviors at work to create an inspiring vision and atmosphere that fosters emotional intelligence in others. In the Navy workshop, we were working on the ability called reflection-in-action—attending to what is happening in the moment in a reflective way, increasing our ability to act according to our judgment of right action, rather than reacting automatically, impulsively, or emotionally.

This way of leadership is challenging because heartfulness demands continual self-reflection and self-growth, through the courage to be vulnerable and to practice on a regular basis.

Perseverance is required in changing old patterns and personal ways of being and acting. This is not easy for those in charge, people with experience, reputations, and titles. Daily mindfulness practice with each new opportunity that arises on the job is a way to raise our emotional intelligence, improve our working relationships, and enhance our leadership capacities.

Beginner's Mind as a Journey Home

Beginner's mind is experienced as a journey that has the uncanny sense of returning to where we started—a way of coming home, of becoming whole. Bringing beginner's mind into my work raises awareness of how I need to live what I teach, practice what I preach. I am challenged to be mindful, to wake up from my dreamlike state to a fuller awareness. Like most people, I am not "present" much of the time, my mind caught up in worries, fears, emotions, and regrets. Being mindful helps us to focus our energies on the present moment. Though we have to attend to both past and future to deal with certain practical things, rather than dwelling there we can center ourselves in the present moment.

I constantly find that I am not really in the present moment but am caught in the past or in the future, not living my present life deeply. Not long ago, I was at a mountain temple in Kyoto, Japan, when I was suddenly overcome with sadness at the thought of my recently deceased dogs and memories of happy times with them and the loss of future times. Sensing what was happening, I focused on my breath, bringing my mind back to my body and being there in the present moment, becoming aware of the beauty of the falling snow amid grand pine trees on the quiet temple grounds. I felt grateful to be there, recognizing the peace that was within and all around me, feeling calm and content. Mindfulness like this offers a way to truly *be* there, waking us to the fact that our lives unfold only in moments and, if we are not fully present for many of those moments, we miss what is most valuable in our lives.

Beginner's mind is a way of being alive, connecting to many principles of the art of conscious living. It's needed every day, for all of us. A mindful consciousness enables us to be more vulnerable, humble, and authentic. We become more appreciative and more grateful. We use mindfulness as the foundation or the gateway to listening, seeing, feeling, connecting. We become better able to accept or change, and to know when one or the other is called for. A mindful condition leads to compassion and responsibility—the way of heartfulness.

Mindfulness has this transformative potential, if taken as more than a self-centered activity that reduces stress and improves well-being for the individual. Research shows that it has the potential to change consciousness in a positive way by leading to more compassionate behavior, perhaps by altering neural functioning in brain areas associated with empathic understanding and felt associations with others.[19] Although the focus appears to be on self, mindfulness can in fact be more than an individual activity with personal benefits, by enhancing attention to others and strengthening awareness of connectedness to all beings. This book will show how heartfulness emphasizes this greater focus, enhancing various principles of living with beginner's mind and mindful consciousness.

EXERCISES

I. *Mindful Observation*

1. Notice and appreciate simple or common elements of your environment with beginner's eyes.
2. Choose a natural object from within your immediate environment and focus on watching it for a minute or two. This could be a tree, a flower, the clouds or moon.
3. Notice the thing you are looking at as if you are seeing it for the first time.
4. Explore every aspect of the thing with all the senses possible—seeing, hearing, smelling, touching, tasting.
5. Imagine connecting with the object's energy and purpose in the natural world.

II. *Mindful Work*

1. Resolve to do activities and tasks mindfully, rather than routinely,

or with an attitude of getting it over as quickly as possible.
2. When you are about to engage in a task, take a brief moment to breathe and focus your attention on what you are doing.
3. Remind yourself of the purpose of your activity, of how it will affect others.
4. Ask yourself to do the job to the best of your ability with any values that might apply, such as patience, kindness, truthfulness.

III. Mindful Email and Social Media

1. Mindful work is also about exercising self-control over habits that increase stress, such as excessively checking email and social media. Unless you are in a situation that demands a constant check, you can decide to check email only at certain designated times.
2. Use a timer to monitor yourself. If you decide on 30 minutes for

checking email, when the timer goes off close your email.
3. Set the timer again for time away from email. Refocus yourself on something else, and resist the urge to check it again until the timer goes off.

For more on bringing balance to our digital lives, see *Mindful Tech* by David M. Levy (New Haven, CT: Yale University Press, 2016).

2
VULNERABILITY

Life is like a long journey with a heavy burden. Let thy step be slow and steady, that thou stumble not. Persuade thyself that imperfection and troubles are the natural lot of mortals, and there will be no room for discontent, neither for despair.... Forbearance is the root of quietness and assurance forever. Look upon the wrath of the enemy. If thou knowest only what it is to conquer, and knowest not what it is like to be defeated, woe unto thee; it will fare ill with thee. Find fault with thyself rather than with others.[1]
—IEYASU TOKUGAWA

I can't remember exactly when, but at some time in my childhood, Saturdays became boxing day in our house. Dad would wait until Mom went out shopping with the girls and, as soon as they were gone, he would jump up, push the table and chairs against the wall, and the lesson would begin.

"Okay, Harry." (He always called me Harry, though my name is Steve. I asked him why once and he said, "I don't know; my name's Fred, but my dad called me Steve.")

"It's all in the left jab," he'd say. "The jab's the key. A good sharp left jab can keep anyone away. Just keep sticking it out, in their face. That's right, snap it, so it jerks their head back." He'd hold out his big laborer's hands and I'd punch them.

"Keep your hands up, protect your face, you're not Ali, don't drop your hands! Okay, then hit him with a quick combination, left, right. Good! Hurt him with the right."

Dad would tell me how sharp my jab was and how it would hold up in any fight, even with a much bigger kid.

I wasn't so sure, but I felt self-confidence in my fighting skills.

"Never start a fight," he said, "but always be ready. Never back down, and if it can't be avoided, look the guy in the eye and say confidently, 'You may win, but I'm gonna hurt you.'"

This all started because I had an obvious vulnerability. Though I was blessed with an able body and mind and was good at most things—school, sports, and music, and was even a "good boy"—I was marked with a visible stigma: I was racially different in a way that others regarded as inferior. This difference could be pointed out at any moment, like at summer camp. I was vulnerable to attacks. I had a weak point that was exploitable if I were to emerge too far into the spotlight. So I walked a fine line between being outstanding without standing out.

While this vulnerability was painful to endure, it freed me from the desire for perfection, as I was obviously imperfect as Japanese, mixed blood, with a mother who was racially different and with an alcoholic, socially dysfunctional father, the only man in town who didn't drive a car. My mixed-race family's marginality constantly reminded me of my imperfection; I couldn't be perfect no matter how hard I tried, so I might as well give up and accept myself.

My mother, a survivor of war and racial hostility, expressed this way of living as *shikata ga nai,* literally "nothing can be done." For me, this meant that you can't change who you are so you better accept it and do what you can with it. So I needed to accept that I was Japanese and make it a source of pride, secretly and intimately held, enabling me to maintain dignity in the face of racial denigration. My father helped by empowering me with stories of my Japanese ancestors, especially the great-grandfather samurai.

Dad sensed the precarious situation I was in and convinced me to accept that I was a target for hostility and to prepare myself for battle as the samurai did. For him, an Irishman—a descendant of colonized people with a fatalistic attitude that disaster was always imminent—this was done by teaching me boxing. He also drilled home the necessity of a calm, mindful presence, always being awake and aware of the threats around me, ready to defend and strike should I be attacked. I had to be unafraid of being hurt, while trusting in my ability to instill fear and inflict damage. This mindset, along with a dramatically violent, public, boxing victory in which I bloodied my opponent's face and sent him off crying, kept attackers at bay. Maybe that was why I was able to endure my summer camp without running away or being beaten. But it also made me guarded and vigilant in my human interactions.

Vulnerability in Japanese Culture

There was a time in my youth when I lived with my grandmother. One day when I was leaving home to go to school in Tokyo, I became sad at the thought of leaving her alone, and said to her, "You'll be lonely, won't you?," acknowledging that she would indeed be lonely without me. But she surprised me by saying, "That's okay, I like loneliness."

We were using the word *sabishii*, which I understood to mean "lonely," but which to my grandmother seemed to have a deeper meaning. Perhaps to her it was the human condition to be lonely, so that being mindful in those moments connected her to others, because we all experience a sadness that is part of life. Hers was a mature acceptance of loneliness, of the fleeting nature of human experience, the suffering in existence—a mellow and peaceful feeling. Loneliness reminds us that we know love. I felt that there was dignity in sacrifice and service in my grandmother's way of doing her part, freeing me to pursue my path.

Sabi represents the material aspects of life, the loss of that which once sparkled, and the fleeting nature of beauty. Like my grandmother, *sabi* things carry the burden of aging with dignity and grace. Although I didn't understand it at the time, her feelings make sense when I realize that the word "sad" comes from the same root as the words "sated" or "satisfied," indicating that it may actually be a kind of fullness—in this case, fullness of heart. We often feel sad when our heart is full, tender, and alive, as opposed to the frozen state of depression that results from pushing away our sadness rather than opening to it.

The expression *wabi sabi* is an aesthetical appreciation of poverty, or absence of materials and material concerns. *Wabi* represents the inner, spiritual experiences of our lives—simple, unmaterialistic, humble by choice, and in tune with nature. Grandmother expressed *wabi* in her satisfaction with simplicity and natural beauty. *Wabi sabi* honors the oddities, the eccentricities, the humble, the unconventional, celebrating the perfectly imperfect uniqueness of you and me and everything. Understanding emptiness while embracing imperfection is honored as a way to cherish our unpolished selves, here and now, just as we are, as the first step to enlightenment.[2]

Wabi sabi is expressed in the ritual of the tea ceremony in which simply making, carrying, serving, and drinking tea is a profound spiritual exercise; sitting in silence conveys mindfulness and acceptance. Harmony, respect, purity, and tranquility are the four most important elements of the tea ceremony, with tranquility being most closely associated with *wabi sabi.*

A related concept, *mono no aware,* expresses compassion and sadness in our awareness of the transience of all things, which in turn deepens our appreciation of their truth or beauty and elicits a gentle sadness at their passing. The love of the glorious yet fleeting beauty of cherry blossoms is characterized by *mono no aware.* This compassionate sensitivity is perhaps what my grandmother was describing.

Another way of appreciating vulnerability is the Japanese art form of imperfection, *kintsugi,* in which pottery is repaired with lacquer mixed with powdered gold. Rather than hiding or disguising the breakages, it treats them as part of the object's history and even illuminates them. *Kintsugi* is related to the philosophy of *mushin,* or "no heart," which evokes a sense of nonattachment to things, accepting the changing and uncontrollable nature of human existence.

Like *kintsugi,* my mixed-race face has served as a reminder of imperfection and the history of my ancestors, helping me to understand *wabi sabi* as mixed-ness, wholeness—both/and rather than either/or. Our imperfection is a way of reminding ourselves that we are all imperfect, freeing us to be authentic. Mixture and imperfection are, after all, fundamental shared qualities of being human.

Awareness of my vulnerability as racially mixed also drew me to others who were stigmatized and targeted for their differences. From high school on, I found meaning in volunteering to work with underprivileged and disabled children, and with people in mental hospitals. I became a special-needs teacher, and then a counselor with Cambodian refugee youth. My vocation became working for the marginalized and oppressed, seeing them as "my people."

While I have continued throughout my career to work for marginalized groups, I realize that vulnerability is part of the human condition that affects us all. There are visible and invisible traumas. When people can be open, feeling respected and listened to, they can share their stories and sense their connectedness with others. Sensing that vulnerability is a key to personal growth and learning, I integrate it into all my formal teaching and my cultivation of human relationships in general.

We experience heartfulness when we allow ourselves be touched by the world and feel the awesome sense of appreciation for others. We find that if we face our demons, we can begin to feel our tenderness, our vulnerability to life, as a living being who is naked to the world, interdependent from and yet connected with all other beings. Moving beyond our judgments and narratives to feel this raw quality of our life relieves suffering. Spirituality means not climbing a ladder of perfection, but rather embracing our wounds, getting in touch with our more basic human tenderness. Vulnerability can be a source of transformative power.

Vulnerability at Harvard

While I was beginning to understand the power of vulnerability in my life, I was greatly surprised to find it taught as an essential element in psychology and medical education at Harvard. I imagined that no one there wanted to risk vulnerability, yet Richard Katz proposed that physicians could benefit from it in their training. At that time, in the 1970s and '80s, it was a radical, pioneering act.

Katz had studied with some of the leading psychologists at Harvard as well as with healers in the Kalahari Desert and in the Fiji islands and with First Nations elders in Saskatchewan. He encouraged us students to own our feelings of vulnerability as real, normal, and even natural.[3] When we made mistakes, didn't know the answers, or felt confused about which direction to take, it didn't indicate failure, but instead affirmed our growing ability to listen to, care for, and help our clients. By loosening our grip on having to be competent, we affirmed our humanity. Accepting our vulnerability as both real and valuable offered us a doorway toward more effective practice as psychologists and scientists.

This was a liberating message for us, as we were constantly reminded by others how elite our program was and felt great pressure to be competent, to know everything, when in reality we all felt vulnerable. Katz's message brought great relief and a sense of "beginner's mind."

Experiencing vulnerability as a prelude to empathy was a source of fear for my fellow students, especially when encountering radically different cultures. I saw that my own reaction to foreignness was, in reality, a reaction to that which I feared within—the realization that we human beings are all essentially flawed. If I'm not able to recognize my own needs, I felt, then I will tend to dismiss others' needs and see them as a threat. Their neediness subconsciously reminded me of my own denied needs.

Entering the world of some clients seemed too dangerous, yet I also saw that the ability to accompany a person wherever their feelings lead is helpful to that person. I felt challenged to suspend my own worldview to allow another, conflicting perspective to be accepted, even valued. I sensed that if I could somehow enter another person's world or culture, and feel exposed to the risks and touched by the joys of that other world, I could learn more about that life.

Katz showed how many spiritual practices cultivate experiences of vulnerability as a necessary prelude to reaching true understanding and connecting with something beyond the individual self. Coming together in community where people share vulnerability is the healing process practiced both in more traditional cultures as well as in support groups in the most modern societies around the world.[4]

I entered the psychology program grounded in what I had learned from East Asian medicine, qigong, Zen, and various indigenous therapies in Japan that focused on how the mind and body works and how to heal from within. My view of Western psychology was that it was good at analyzing but had both an incomplete understanding of human nature and an unrealistic expectation of a practitioner's ability to actually promote health and well-being. I saw that I needed to open myself to the world of biomedical and experimental science, respecting that view while presenting mine with clarity and integrity. That would enable respectful collaboration as well as an exchange of knowledge.

As my practice of psychotherapy developed, I recognized in my clients the fear, rawness, and tenderness they felt when facing a catastrophic loss. They were confronted with the reality of their humanness that they normally mask to protect themselves either from feeling vulnerable or from being perceived as too emotional or weak.

When they were able to open up and risk making themselves vulnerable, it created the possibility of receiving something that enriched their emotional life, giving purpose and meaning to living. They learned that vulnerability is hard to face but is the source of deeper, more meaningful human relations and work. Through their life experiences they found that strength appears to be weakness, and that very weakness is actually where their strength lies. They had to be strong enough to allow themselves to be vulnerable, to live with their hearts as well as their minds, in a state of openness, integrating what they know intellectually with what they know experientially.

In my own life, including my youthful summer camp experience described earlier, I saw that the key to transforming vulnerability into *courage* is learning how to recognize and accept my vulnerable feelings, facing and embracing them. If I can be mindful, slow down and breathe, know what I'm feeling and why, I can make choices that accept and reflect who I am and what I believe. Then the door to profound self-knowledge opens, to an important source of valid data and learning that comes by seeing from inside one's experience, from within one's knowledge of oneself. I began to recognize the profound truth that, for society to function, it must educate its members to understand and accept their own vulnerability.

Another Harvard professor from whom I learned about vulnerability was Chester Pierce. I first encountered him as I sat in his class on how to treat psychological disorders of people of color. But Dr. Pierce surprised us by telling us to look at ourselves first. That was not what most of us wanted to hear. Yes, we sought competence in working with patients who were culturally or racially different and less fortunate than us, but we thought it would be easier than it turned out to be. We truly desired to help them, yet unconsciously didn't want to examine our motives. We were there to learn about *them,* not *us.*

Several students in his class became irritated and impatient. "Please tell me," one audacious student finally demanded, "only what I need to know to treat my patients. What do I need to know about African Americans or Vietnamese immigrants?" The look on Dr. Pierce's face told me he had heard this request before. He calmly told us that we should learn what we can about the experiences of others, but warned us, "People cannot tell you what is great or awful about being who they are. The best way to understand another is to understand your own experience. Ask yourself, 'What do I know about the trials, tribulations, and consciousness unique to my experience that others may not?' Since it's impossible to understand everything about all other cultures, you need to learn what you can about your own group and use it as a basis of understanding others."

Many of my fellow students struggled with accepting this lesson, wanting their study to be objective, scientific, detached, even spoon-fed. They didn't want to be vulnerable, despite Dr. Pierce's warning that our own racial or class background limited our understanding of the realities of a patient's life. When we saw paranoia in a patient, he cautioned us to be careful in our diagnosis because people of color have historical reasons to be defensive, uptight, even seemingly paranoid, because of past discriminatory events and expectations of being used or treated poorly.

Dr. Pierce forced us to confront our vulnerability by telling us that we needed to be aware that we are often perceived by our patients as condescending and controlling and that our competence is questioned. He warned us that people of color have reason to be skeptical that doctors have at best only an 8-to-5-o'clock interest in them.

We learned that the worlds in which many people of color live are highly stressful, extreme environments in which they are ridiculed, dehumanized, even terrorized. Constant exposure to what Dr. Pierce termed "offensive mechanisms" and "microaggressions," seemingly insignificant acts readily dismissed as trivial by others, was actually profoundly destructive in its cumulative effect.[5] He showed us how, when delivering microaggressions, the oppressor takes the offense, initiating and terminating contact and controlling the action. The oppressed person is put on the defensive, forced to think about many more things, be highly vigilant, and use greater energy, to the detriment of their health.

We knew that as an African-American Harvard undergrad and medical student, athlete, professor, and naval officer, Dr. Pierce had had profound personal experiences. He shared them judiciously with his students to show how people of color must yield time, space, and energy to the oppressor. We winced when he told us of the time, when he was dressed in a sparkling white garment denoting his elite profession, a patient asked if he was the barber. He taught us of internalized oppression he observed in his own family when, one week before his Harvard Medical School graduation, his hospitalized aunt complained to him about her attending physician, saying, "You know, Chester, colored doctors don't know anything."

I myself experienced vulnerability in my training in a hospital in the black community of Roxbury, a suburb of Boston, where I confronted the reality of how I was perceived by my fellow workers. The secretary, who befriended me, confided in me that I was referred to sarcastically by the other doctors, as "the Harvard guy." And the

Asian-American identity I presented was directly challenged by a supervisor who asked how my patients liked having a "white doctor," though she quickly corrected herself and said, "I mean, I know you're Asian, but you look white!"

When I got the opportunity to teach at the Stanford School of Medicine many years later, I drew on Dr. Pierce's teachings in designing a program of "cultural humility." This method encourages health care providers to enhance patient care by adopting an attitude of learning about the cultures, worldviews, and realities of life for their patients rather than needing to be the ultimate expert. Cultural humility focuses on our developing a greater understanding of our own cultural backgrounds, experiences, and worldviews by becoming aware of our assumptions, values, and prejudices about our fellow humans and their behavior.[6] Practicing self-reflection and mindfulness in our work enables us to notice our reactions and attitudes toward our patients and then to correct them. We see that understanding and accepting others is ultimately about understanding and accepting ourselves.

Students learn the importance of not knowing, of how to handle failures, and of admitting and accepting their mistakes. Including their appreciation of experiences of vulnerability in their formal education can help people in many fields to accept their own fallibility and to open themselves to new learning opportunities.

Stanford Duck Syndrome

From 2003 on, I spent a few years at Stanford as a faculty fellow, residing next door to 60 students, eating, playing, and working with them. I got to see their lives up close and learned that the "Duck Syndrome" was real. On the surface, a duck glides along the pond effortlessly, appearing serene, calm, and still. However, under the water the duck is actually paddling intensely. Often students similarly appear to have everything under control, and feel supremely satisfied and happy, yet inside some are struggling mightily to stay alive and afloat. They make a good impression and feel secure by avoiding risks, defending themselves with an air of self-confidence, self-control, and independence.

These youths strive for perfection and have been greatly rewarded for their achievement. Many have rarely, if ever, failed, yet they are afraid of failing, feeling that they cannot afford to make mistakes. For some, their first big mistake can completely derail them.

They are flying high with their inflated egos, intellectualizing everything, living in their heads, heavily invested in their achievements. Wanting what is safe and predictable forces them into a pattern of learning that dulls them to new ways of knowledge.

I find their level of emotional disturbance to be alarming, reflecting a phenomenon across the country of high rates of mental illness among college students. Conversely, we also see a growing desire for spirituality and disillusionment with the lack of this guidance in colleges. To respond to these needs, my colleagues and I designed a program called Life-Works, a series of courses to help students deal with the most urgent and profound questions in their lives.

Our heartful approach first disrupts students' assumptions about what will happen in the class, asking them to bring beginner's mind and openness to the possibility of learning something important for their lives. The hope is that they will stop taking things for granted, will question, and will admit what they know may not be true. They need to realize how much they don't know and recognize the great strength of humility that comes with being honest with themselves and accepting their weaknesses.

I model vulnerability in my classes and workshops, subtly suggesting that this is an experience that will lead us to deep discoveries. There are many ways to do this, less dramatic than speaking Japanese, and each teacher can find their own way. I may simply explain who I am and why I am there. Even this level of openness stands in stark contrast to the orthodox approach of teaching with detached objectivity. As one professor explained to me, at the moment of crossing the threshold of the classroom, "We leave ourselves at the door." Instead, I aspire to what the great conductor and educator Leonard Bernstein described as the state in which when we are teaching, we are also learning; when we are learning, we are also teaching. He noted that "teacher" and "learner" in both German and Yiddish are nearly the same word, being interconnected and inseparable.[7]

I encourage students to experience vulnerability by letting go of the need to have opinions about everything, to appear invincible to others, directing their attention to where they fear most to look. They can do this by being in touch with and appropriately open about their feelings. Developing a sense of vulnerability, humility, and equality enables students to quickly abandon their customary desires to compete and compare, to prove that they are better than others, and to cover their perceived weaknesses. They are then freed to be accepting and appreciative of others' competence, giving themselves more energy for creativity, new discoveries, and connections with others. Embracing vulnerability and humility, engaging in mindful self-reflection, they become empty, listening, open, and receptive to learning. Research studies show that the students who think they know the least study more when given a problem, and are more efficient than those who think they already have the answer.[8] They work harder and prepare themselves better, balancing a sense of competence with humility.

In heartful communities, mindfulness enhances our ability to be vulnerable and open to embracing our imperfection. By paying attention to moments of vulnerability, we can learn to trust in ourselves, feeling empowered to observe what we are experiencing when we are emotionally vulnerable and embrace an open, accepting, nonjudgmental attitude. We are more capable of remaining present when something challenging and threatening arises, even things against which we may have spent years defending ourselves.

I have seen the positive effects of mindfully connecting with our vulnerability with low-achieving children, high-achieving college students, and adults of all kinds. People everywhere are afraid to embrace vulnerability and learn new things. Many of us feel inadequate but get out of touch with our true feelings, hiding behind a shield of willful strength. Heartfulness is a way of developing the belief that growth is possible by embracing vulnerability.

Those who have had less academic success find it hard to summon the courage to make the attempt to learn and thereby to risk failure. They are often actually capable but feel beaten down by an educational system that has robbed them of their motivation, curiosity, and self-confidence. They have not been seen or heard and thus are labeled as deficient. Cynical about ever being recognized for their ability, they would rather play it safe and hide out in silence in the back of the room.

When I studied with Stanford professor Carol Dweck at Harvard in the 1980s, she was at the beginning stages of her research on how people can get stuck in a belief that their basic abilities, intelligence, and talents are fixed traits, what she later called a "fixed mindset." In this mindset we just want to look as good as we can and to avoid looking stupid. We don't take chances, yet if we can risk being vulnerable, we can come to nurture a "growth mindset," believing that our talents and abilities can be developed through effort, persistence, and good teaching.

To help people become vulnerable and develop a growth mindset, I sometimes perform a story concerning a Buddhist scholar and a Zen master. I play the master and a student plays the scholar, who has an extensive background in Buddhist studies and who comes to study with the master and, after making the customary bows, asks the master to teach him Zen. But the student starts talking about his extensive scholarly background and rambles on and on about the many sutras he has studied, showing the master how much he knows.

The master listens patiently and then begins to make tea. When it is ready, he pours the tea into the scholar's cup until it begins to overflow and run all over the floor. The scholar sees what is happening and shouts, "Stop, stop!

The cup is full; you can't get any more in."

The master stops pouring and says: "You are like this cup; you are full of ideas about Buddha's Way. You come and ask for teaching, but your cup is full; I can't put anything in. Before I can teach you, you'll have to empty your cup."

The story impresses young people who are already closed to learning new things, filled with their own ideas and opinions and trapped by their conditioning, unable to absorb life lessons when they encounter them. They find it difficult to empty themselves, having been brought up to value rational thought processes above all else—an attitude deeply embedded and drilled home in most school systems. Reason is considered superior to emotion or feelings of the heart.

Embracing vulnerability challenges this dominance of the intellect, opening us to be guided by our heart, by our whole being. Heart conveys a sense of affectivity. In the Latin origin of the word "affectivity," *affectus,* we see not merely feeling but also a state of openness in which we are vulnerable to the world outside us. This state of openness expands with mindfulness.

Vulnerability and Parenting

We can approach parenting similarly, by valuing vulnerability, as in the summer camp story. I realize that my dad gave me a great gift that day. Even though he may have felt disappointed that I had failed at my great adventure, he didn't show it. He let me be vulnerable and frail, accepting me with my weaknesses. He let me be the little boy that I was, scared and hurt, and he comforted me; that gave me the courage to go on. My father's tender compassion guided my parenting of my own boys, trusting that they, too, will find courage in accepting their vulnerability.

When adults accept children's vulnerability, it becomes easier for them to accept their feelings and get through their tough experiences. If we are comfortable with our children's weaknesses and tenderness, they will be too, discovering that they can in fact survive difficult and painful feelings, trusting in their ability to be strong. Though modern cultures teach us that vulnerability equals weakness, parents can give children the message that acceptance of weakness is a sign of maturity. We show fearlessness in the willingness to open to whatever we're experiencing.

My father also dramatically demonstrated his vulnerability, particularly under the influence of alcohol, declaring himself a failure who did not succeed in life. He painted himself as a dreamer, an idealist, who could not adjust to the real world and could only work as a manual laborer. He showed me this so that I would take a different path, be more like my mother, who was the model of success, extremely pragmatic and efficient. His vulnerability was hard for me to deal with as a child and an adolescent, and later in life he expressed regret that he had burdened me with a negative view of life. I did, however, learn compassion for the human condition that guides my work with people suffering. I also learned the flexibility to adapt to life by taking on unconventional, possibly more authentic gender roles, as he did at times, in becoming the nurturing, domestic parent.

I have been more cautious as a parent, letting my children trust in my public image of success, but even now I am discovering that moments of vulnerability can create openings in relationships with children. When my son's dog was dying, he was away at college, so I called to tell him. I was overcome with sadness as I explained that death was imminent. In that moment, there was a rawness and tenderness that prompted me to tell him that "though I never say, 'I love you,' you know I do." I confessed that as a parent I can't tell him what to do, because I messed up so much myself, and did all the stupid things he does. He was clearly moved by my revelation of vulnerability, and it seemed to spark a change in him and a search for his path in life.

Sensei

In my role as teacher, I seek to model vulnerability by accepting that I am responsible and accountable, but also seeing myself as simply a fellow human who is further along the path than my younger students, and still searching for truth and beauty. I teach what I need to learn, seeking to embody the things I teach in everyday life.

I suggest that students call me *"sensei,"* commonly used for "teachers," and explain the meaning as revealed in the *kanji* 先生. The term 先 means to precede; 生 means to live; so the two, combined, simply mean "One who lives before you," and are an expression of respect for an elder as one who has experienced life and is walking further down the road. Relieving myself of the burden of imagining that I am an elder imparting wisdom to others, I seek to become one who listens, asks questions, and tells stories. I offer my presence and I trust in my students to live with whatever experiences arise in their lives.

On a recent visit to a Zen Buddhist temple in Japan, I was asked by a monk what I do for a living. I gave him the usual answers—I'm a college professor; I teach psychology. But after meditating at the temple, I saw him again on the way out and gave him a different answer. I told him that I really don't teach anything; I just bring myself to the place where my students gather and stay with them the best I can—mindful, vulnerable, authentic.

Being vulnerable with students is not commonly done, though it offers a deep form of learning, according to feminist bell hooks:

> The teacher also has to be a person who is going a little further. I don't for a minute think that we can be teachers who invite students into radical openness if we're not willing to be radically open ourselves, if we're not willing to be a witness to our students of how ideas change and shape us, how something affects us so that we think differently than we did before.[9]

My call for students to be open to the recognized *sensei* in their lives extends to the possibility of their seeing the *sensei* in *everyone,* learning from each person they meet, each one deserving respect and possessing knowledge that only they have. In this way of viewing knowledge, it becomes unlimited and expandable and is possessed by and is to be shared by all. This is synergy in which the whole is greater than the sum of its parts.

I believe that when we are open to others, we learn from all beings, including animals, so I sometimes bring my dogs to class. If we approach each encounter with vulnerability, being receptive to what is happening at that moment, we can see ourselves and everything as fresh and new. We are able to receive things with an open mind, empty of preconceptions and unburdened by what has happened in the past. As in the previous Zen story of emptying the cup with humility, we are able to meet every moment and be filled by it, an ability cultivated in the practice of mindfulness.

Humility also affects the way we relate with others. The word comes from the same Latin roots as *human*, so if we are humble, an encounter can honor the existence of the other person as another human being, just like us. Looking at people judgmentally, thinking they have nothing to teach us, closes us to truly seeing them and listening to them. If we are humble, we recognize that all around us are people who can enrich us by sharing their lives. When people embrace vulnerability, it creates heartful spaces that have a sense of *wabi sabi,* bringing mindful attention and appreciation to the "flawed beauty" of human beings.

Relating deeply with others means risking being open and transparent, while appreciating and taking an interest in what they are experiencing and how they are different from oneself. This capacity for open expressiveness and deep attunement is extremely rare in this world, and is especially difficult if you are relationally wounded, like many of us. Heartful communities offer the possibility of being healing spaces based in mutual respect, unconditional positive regard, and nonjudgmental listening.

Some people with experiences of trauma need extra safety and cannot be simply told "this is a safe space!" nor even lightly encouraged to "be vulnerable." Safety must be created through mutual vulnerability. If our space is truly safe, we can each reveal ourselves authentically. With even one word expressed, like "sad," we call forth humility, gratitude, acceptance, and forgiveness. Others then eagerly tell stories of when they have been driven to their knees and humbled by hard times.

We can reflect on how the gift of humility greets us in our most difficult moments, those times when we realize our humanness, frailty, fallibility, and vulnerability. If we manage not to be overwhelmed by our defeats, they will show us what we can and cannot do.

Like many others, I often rely on nature to keep me humble. Even for just a moment, simply gazing at the stars at night reminds me who I am in relation to an infinitely vast universe, one among billions on this planet, which is itself no more than a speck of dust in the universe. Each life is just a moment in the vastness of time. This awareness heartens me to embrace my vulnerability, accepting myself as both a tiny part of life and an integral part of an infinite universe.

EXERCISES

I. Imperfect Is Perfect

Acknowledging our imperfections helps us to accept ourselves as we are.
1. Reflect on what you consider your weaknesses, and write them down.
2. Close your eyes and take three deep breaths, inhaling deeply and exhaling slowly.
3. Tell yourself three times, "I'm doing my best. I don't need to be perfect."
4. Open your eyes and look at your list, noticing how you now feel about each item.

II. Learning from Setbacks

Reflective writing about our lives can enable us to realize how seemingly negative things can be the source of our greatest lessons in life.
1. Reflect on a time in your life that you regard as a failure, a setback, a mistake, a misfortune, or a rejection.

2. What did you learn or gain from the experience?
3. How are you a better person today as a result of that experience?
4. Write down your thoughts for 10 minutes.

3
AUTHENTICITY

If I didn't define myself for myself, I would be crunched into other people's fantasies for me and eaten alive.[1]

—AUDRE LORDE

When I was 10 years old we moved from a small city to a neighboring town in Massachusetts. The kids were really fascinated by me, because they'd never encountered an Asian before in real life. It didn't bother them at all that I was only "half"; they thought I was the real deal.

One Saturday, some of the boys went to see *Blue Hawaii,* Elvis Presley's latest film. I wasn't invited. On Monday when I went to school they had a surprise for me—a new nickname.

I knew it wasn't going to be Elvis but was dumbstruck when they gleefully announced they had found the perfect name for me—Ping Pong! Johnny explained that I reminded them of Elvis's Chinese servant who, naturally, was named Ping Pong. Billy said it was just the best possible name for me. I wanted to tell them it was no good because I was Japanese, not Chinese, but knew it wouldn't make any difference. I was saddled with Ping Pong for years, though they did mercifully shorten it to Ping.

I finally saw *Blue Hawaii* recently and understood the dire situation I faced as a child. Elvis calls his adult servant "boy," and Ping Pong is a grinning fool, a little, harmless pet who serves the giant, beautiful white men and women. I realized that I had made a pact with myself to never be that "boy," to never grovel. It was life and death to me. Somehow, I let everyone know that if they dared to threaten me with violence they might win, but that I would not go down without a fight, in which they would be hurt. In my room, all alone, I honored my Japanese heritage to maintain my dignity, hiding a little national flag in the back of a desk drawer.

This racial and national identity struggle colored my American socialization. A strange part of growing up in the United States was that others were extremely interested in me. They thought I looked different, and some were disturbed enough to say things expressing their dislike of who they thought I was. Or they asked questions to help them figure out who I was. The nature of their treatment was sometimes wounding and traumatizing, leading to growing self-consciousness and a consuming struggle about my identity.

Their mostly negative and derogatory reactions forced a confrontation with what it meant to be Japanese. It was apparent that my life would be easier if I weren't Japanese but was white like nearly everyone else around me. My mother's response to the situation was a message of stoic self-acceptance, assuring me that I was as good or better than others, and that accepting who I was would strengthen me. This helped me to just be myself.

My father's stories of my samurai great-grandfather had the powerful effect of enabling me to reject internalizing "Ping Pong." Outwardly, I was a gentle boy, but when my safety was threatened, I embodied the internalized self of my cool, calm samurai great-grandfather. This became clearer to me when I read of how bell hooks had as a child rejected the good, little black girl she was supposed to be and instead adopted the persona of her outspoken, rebellious great-grandmother.[2] Though I may not have discovered my real, authentic self in taking on a samurai identity, it was the only one available to me in my cultural setting other than Ping.

Yet there was more to deal with than just individual assaults. While I was highly visible, I never saw anyone who looked like me on television or in movies. There were so few images of people like me that the other kids took the only ones they saw and branded me as a "Jap," or as "Ping." This kind of treatment tested my Japanese identity, tempting me to wish to escape the imprisonment of my heritage. I struggled with accepting who I was. I knew that breaking the psychological chains of internalized victimhood was not done by identifying with the oppressor, but this thought remained private, not declared publicly.

By the time I was a teenager, I couldn't wait to get out of my small, white town. My parents could see my anguish and told me it would be okay to go away. I found that there were prep schools that were giving financial aid scholarships. I got one and went off to join the sons of the rich and famous. When I and my family got to my assigned room at school we were first greeted by an odd fellow who seemed like the typical rich, white preppie I was expecting, but we were surprised when in walked my other roommate, who introduced himself as Rap Brown. Rap was one of several black kids from the inner cities who were on scholarships. His real first name was Percelle, but he called himself Rap after his hero, H. Rap Brown, the Black Panther.

Rap and I got along well. We shared everything and he introduced me to the other black students. I became like an honorary member of their group. They shared their music—Aretha, The Temptations, Marvin, Tammy—and their books, *Invisible Man, Native Son, The Autobiography of Malcolm X.* They taught me how to dance. Rap even shared his Afro picks, which I didn't really need.

One day I dropped by to see Rap at the store inside the gym locker room where he worked. He was reading a book, titled *Black Rage.* We chatted a bit and then he got this wicked gleam in his eye and disappeared into the back of the store. He came back with a box, which I quickly noticed were Converse All Stars, size 10—my size.

When I saw them, I said, "Oooh, Cons!" I'd always wanted a pair of Cons.

Rap mumbled, "Take 'em," and shoved them toward me.

I said, "What? You know I can't pay for them."

"Take 'em," he repeated, and when I hesitated, he added, "We know you're on scholarship, just like us."

I looked around and no one was there. So I grabbed the Cons and fled out the door. I got back to my room, shut the door, and tried on my first pair of Cons. They fit perfectly. I was confused. I'd been taught not to steal, but I'd done it anyway. I even thought that maybe it was okay.

I'd been included by the black kids *because* I was Japanese, and it was totally different than the way my white friends had *overlooked* the fact that I was Japanese. Now it was what connected me. And Rap had included me because I wasn't one of the rich kids. It was an amazing feeling, both of being united with others who didn't have as much as some people and of seeing that by working together we could get what we needed and, if we didn't, we could take it.

At graduation, some of my white classmates made something they called individual "Class Wills." These were announced at graduation. Mine was supposed to be funny. "Steve Murphy leaves ... ALMOST BLACK." I looked out in the crowd and saw my parents sitting there amid the nervous laughter that erupted. My dad, the son of an Irish laborer and a house maid, a so-called "Black Irish," a laborer himself dressed in his Sunday suit and wingtip shoes sitting among bankers, doctors, and lawyers. My mom, an immigrant Asian woman, in her makeup, high heels, and Western dress, sticking out in the sea of white faces. My parents may have felt disappointed, but I wasn't. I was living the values they taught me, and I left that school knowing better who I was, with more respect for Mom and Dad—and more respect for myself.

I thought of how much my life had changed since I had come to the school. I was no longer the "Ping" of my small town. I knew I wasn't Chinese. And though the white kids saw me their way, I knew I wasn't "almost black." And I also knew I wasn't white—I had been told that long enough. I knew who I wasn't, but I was just discovering who I *was*. Though I was romanticizing, and the samurai identification may not have been my authentic self, I was developing what the psychologist Erik Erikson describes as a sense of identity involving experiences of an increased unity and oneness in the way one experiences oneself and the way others experience us.[3]

Racial experiences had instilled compassion in me as well as in others who felt that we "suffered together" in a white world. We felt responsible for each other. This was a formative moment in my personal development of heartfulness.

In my imagination, I was the Irish-Japanese Celtic samurai. But I was still searching—for a surrendered identity, my roots, my wings, my place in the human family, my community. And I knew I was on my way home.

Homecoming

Even though I had lived in Japan just a short time, in a strange way it had become home for me. Amid the American kids, I was the only one constantly identified as Tokyo born, "made in Japan," like the derogatory label at the time for cheap products. After college, lost in the fog of youth, with no idea how to move forward, a light shined through for me with a clarity I have never experienced before or since. The message I was receiving was, "return home." To me this meant to my birthplace, my roots in Japan, in what I now see as a way to find authenticity, the "real me." I sensed that I would discover something there that I could not even imagine.

As I wrote in the preface, this became a transformative journey of self-discovery. I was empowered to act in ways that created a new life. Reunited with my grandparents in the city of Matsuyama, with a beginner's mind, I learned Japanese language and culture as well as a way of living and being. I found that these were already part of me, my authentic self, and living in this way was both natural and genuine, bringing a sense of wholeness.

My grandmother, who would live past 111, was a woman of tremendous life energy. Being with her, I absorbed some of that energy and became empowered to act courageously. My mother was her only child, and I was her only grandson. She raised me like the son she had never had, teaching me as if I were her child. Grandmother convinced me I had a purpose in life—that I had been given certain things through my ancestors and that they walked with me. I had responsibilities to them, to myself, and to the world. My task was to fulfill my purpose.

So, I have devoted my life to finding and living it. I realized that my task was to be mindful of moments in which I feel that I am experiencing insight into my purpose. Listening carefully and then acting courageously is challenging. But doing so is how we embrace our unique self or authenticity.

Reflecting deeply on my life circumstances, I saw clearly that I existed because two people came together following a tragic war in which they were on opposing sides. They crossed borders in declaring their love and determination to be together, despite legal and social barriers. Seeing myself in this way, I imagined that this was my purpose—to play my part in bringing people of these two countries together. Its practical expression lay in becoming a doctor who promoted the integration of medicine and the healing of East and West.

Believing that I had a purpose in life, being the real me, gave me tremendous energy. I realized that authentic living was not important solely for me but was important for others, as well. The feeling that my actions were taken not only for my own happiness or success, but more for some greater good, was liberating. This knowledge helped me to overcome self-consciousness and fear and move out into the world with the assurance that I was not alone but was supported by many others and perhaps even by some greater spiritual power. I eventually left my grandparents' home, empowered to do what I could in the world, and entered Harvard University with the goal of fulfilling my purpose.

This idea that my life has purpose was strengthened by a profound message expressed by Albert Einstein:

> How strange is the lot of us mortals! Each of us is here for a brief sojourn; for what purpose he knows not, though he sometimes thinks he senses it.[4]

To me this meant mindfully discovering and surrendering to what I can understand as my purpose. I believed that if I was dedicated to doing so, then somehow I would know what it was that I was to do. I decided to go on this journey, to live authentically in the creation of my life.

I started to see the true self as myself at birth—who I was born to be. If I was able to simply be who I am, I could grow into my potential. I saw that my mission, and indeed everyone's, was to live into my true self, and that this is done not by comparing ourselves to others but by accepting who we truly are. We each have a part to play, a purpose that no one else can fulfill; we are needed as we are. Like every person, we are incomparably unique. When we feel self-acceptance and appreciation for who we truly are, we feel alive, sensing our purpose, doing what needs to be done in leading a full and meaningful life.

Who Are You?

In the classes I teach, our search for authenticity begins with a "Who Are You?" exercise that helps students to see how difficult it is to answer such a simple question if we try to say who we are without using the common descriptors of our affiliations, status, and achievements. We confront the disturbing reality that we don't really *know* who we are. This helps students to see that they need to know who they are because, if they don't, someone else will tell them. But that person will always be wrong, because we know ourselves in a way that no one else can. While others may see parts of us that we cannot even see ourselves, there will always be an inner voice that only we can hear that tells us who we truly are. The challenge is to discover our true, authentic self, by engaging in a continual process of building self-awareness, a journey through which we acknowledge our strengths and limitations, and identify our purpose.

How we find authenticity differs for each of us. For some people it comes through meditation; for someone else it is through nature; and for another it is by caring for the suffering and the needy. Some find it in work, others through art, music, or prayer. We all have our way of reconnecting with the healthy, true self, but we have to discover it, which is a great adventure. The journey to self-awareness gives the foundation of emotional intelligence, as there is no more important task than to know oneself.

Discovering our authentic self is, however, no easy task. We feel that we can discover authenticity in special moments when we sense our words and actions emerging mysteriously from deep inside us. We may surprise ourselves with the awareness that we are new every moment. This sensation is supported by research that provides evidence of how mindfulness can lead to changes in behavior and brain physiology, creating a new you, so that each moment is a new opportunity to re-create yourself.[5]

Even if we are constantly evolving, there is still a sense of connecting to some essence that feels real. Bringing forth authentic selves begins by being mindful and engaging in a process of deep self-reflection, and then living within the flow of our awareness, in our most natural state of existence. We become more able to ask ourselves basic questions and to listen to the answer we hear from the deep, inner voice.

This process requires belief that there is an authentic self, a true and unique identity, hidden behind fears, doubts, and worries. It is waiting to be discovered as a doorway to a meaningful life. Authenticity lies deep within. You know when you touch it, and those around you also recognize it.

William James, the father of American psychology, encourages us to "Seek out that particular mental attribute which makes you feel most deeply and vitally alive, along with which comes the inner voice which says, 'This is the real me,' and when you have found that attitude, follow it."[6]

I experienced this a few years ago at a seminar conducted by a prominent person in the field of healing and storytelling. She opened a session by saying that she was required by the state of California to do something about cultural competence. I heard her saying that we would do it even if we didn't really need to, as if we had already transcended those kinds of things. I felt stunned and looked around the room and saw a sea of white, smiling faces nodding, as if in agreement that they really didn't need to be trained in cultural competence but were willing to go along with it. I felt dissonance, out of place, different from the others.

I was awakened to feeling "deeply and vitally alive," with a voice telling me "this is the real me." What was of great concern to me at that moment, what I felt was the focus of much of my life, was being dismissed in importance. I could see where I might play a role in expanding the mindfulness movement through a heartful approach that is inclusive, values diversity, and promotes social justice.

Find What You Love; Love What You Do

Many students have been influenced by the words of Steve Jobs, the late Apple CEO, who in 2005 delivered one of the most popular commencement speeches in Stanford University history, five years before his untimely death. He explained that he quit college because he realized that he was simply doing what others expected of him, following the mainstream. But after dropping out he discovered that new things were possible by wandering off the conventional path in life. His stories of finding purpose are inspiring for young people trying to understand who they are and what they want to do, but Jobs warned that the path to authenticity is steep, requiring courage and trust:

> You've got to find what you love; and that is as true for work

as it is for your lovers. Your work is going to fill a large part of your life and the only way to be truly satisfied is to do what you believe is great work, and the only way to do great work is to love what you do. If you haven't found it yet, keep looking, don't settle. As with all matters of the heart, you'll know when you find it and like any great relationship it just gets better and better as the years roll on. So keep looking, don't settle.[7]

The message to "keep looking, don't settle" continues to resonate with young people who have the resources to pursue their dreams. One student told me how he had done everything that was expected of him, never stopping to ask, "Does this fit my sense of who I am? Is this truly my gift and my calling?" Yet he came to feel depressed, realizing how his inability to listen to his inner voice had left him in a place of deep pain. When he finally listened and began taking in and acting on the self-knowledge, he took his first steps on the path to well-being.

The way Steve Jobs talks of finding an authentic self is inspiring and appealing, yet some of my students have a hard time with it. In one class, after I introduced Jobs' message, which was followed by another message from a male CEO in Silicon Valley, some students expressed their discomfort and difficulty relating to being taught about life from these people of power and privilege.

These students noticed that there is no mention of the self beyond the individual. They resonate with the view of social justice advocate john powell, who writes about how the Western self, and especially the American self, is particularly isolated and separate, rooted in a history of ideals that assert a radical individualism.[8] He sees the need for an alternative vision, a beloved community where being connected to the other is seen as a foundation of a healthy self. This is a self that is based in the recognition of shared vulnerabilities rather than egoistic separateness.

How we see ourselves as authentic and find a sense of purpose for our life is related to our culture's views of the self. The independent way of viewing the self differs radically from the view in many cultures—that of a self in relation, a self dependent on others. This self is not defined by increased autonomy gained by separating oneself from others, but rather as self found in the context of family and community. The ways that such cultures view the self are constantly evolving. The popular individualistic and collectivistic duality disguises the existence of complex values in each individual.

People in Japan, for example, have learned to submerge a self to conform to group norms, yet there is another self that longs for expressions of individuality. When Yuko Arimoto, who won a silver medal for the marathon at the 1992 Olympics and a bronze medal in the Olympics four years later, made the public statement "I'd like to congratulate myself," I believe that she was voicing the unexpressed sentiment of many Japanese.[9]

The sense of self affects our beliefs in the importance of happiness. Psychologists are increasingly emphasizing the importance of living a meaningful life rather than one focused merely on achieving happiness.[10] Happiness is self-centered, focused on receiving, having your needs satisfied, getting what you want, and feeling good. Meaning is more related to developing a personal identity, expressing the self, and consciously integrating one's past, present, and future experiences.[11]

A key to our search for meaningful work is a sense of purpose, as it is associated with increased retention, productivity, and satisfaction.[12] We find purpose in two ways: connection to something greater and making a difference in someone's life, or service. Business leaders declare that a purpose is important for their organization, but they struggle with knowing how to think about defining it clearly or helping their companies act on it.[13]

A philosophy of finding purpose in work is offered by Jiro Ono, the subject of the film *Jiro Dreams of Sushi,* who asserts, "You have to love your job. Once you decide on your occupation you must immerse yourself in your work. You have to fall in love with your work. Never complain about your job. You must dedicate your life to mastering your skill; that is the secret of success and key to being regarded honorably." His clear message is that to love your work can at times be difficult and that you may have to sacrifice, but that if you persevere you will find yourself rewarded for it.

While many people in the world may see reality in Ono's view, those who have privileges of higher education and career opportunities may see it as a dream killer. They are drawn to the individualistic emphasis on finding the self and following the heart, as Steve Jobs advocates. Yet they may sense that the focus on adjusting to reality is also valuable, necessary, and meaningful. When we think about who we are and how to follow our heart, both dimensions must be considered. All of us must care for ourselves, as well as for others.

Discovering our unique purpose in life is a difficult, challenging task because each of us is at once an individual and part of something larger than ourself. Our purpose will be to honor our inner voice and follow our heart in fulfilling our needs both as individuals and as members of broader circles. We are part of a larger whole and can see ourselves in this complexity. Finding our passion, or an ideal job, or an authentic self, may be as elusive as finding a life partner. Each of us can try to find this authentic self, which is our unique calling. Then we decide what kinds of sacrifices we're willing to make, knowing that what we are called to do may not be what we would have chosen.

Whether or not you are Christian, there is a powerful image in our Western culture of Jesus in the Garden of Gethsemane praying to God the night before his crucifixion, asking, "Father, if you are willing, please take this cup of suffering away from me. Yet I want your will to be done, not mine." Similarly, we ask ourselves if we can generate the kind of courage to act boldly and fearlessly on what we feel called to do. While the path we have chosen may initially lead to survival, it may also lead to sacrifice.

A few people are idealists and will naturally follow their heart. They feel they have a purpose, or a mission, and they go for it, come what may. They may succeed or they may crash and burn. Some may do both during their lifetimes.

We all have this option of daring to follow the compassionate ideal and to say that there is no difference between us and others in the world, and then to live as if that was true. But how many of us can overcome our fears of what might happen if we really practiced our ideals and followed our dreams? Are we able to imagine our lives if we were truly heroic and did "God's will," even when it is a treacherous path? How many of us will commit to being truly compassionate, or always being courageous?

Some of us will not listen to our own heart. Or we may listen and decide that the path is too steep and so we choose another, safer trail. We may pay a price for this, living with regrets for not following our heart. Most of us will seek a decent life that is reasonably prosperous and secure and is oriented to family and stability. We will try to take care of ourselves and also care for others. For many of us, a heartful way of living may mean to try to balance our ideals with realism, peacefully holding two seemingly contradictory truths in mind at the same time.

We actually live in the middle, between two worlds. It takes constant effort and daily practice to stay on the path of heartfulness. We can try to live up to ideals and also accept being authentically who we are and where we are. Neuroscience research tells us that while our character is formed early in life, we are more malleable than we imagined and can actually form a new self each moment.[14] We live in this tension between two realities of who we are. This question is also experienced in our need to determine what in life needs to be accepted and what can be changed, in ourselves and in life in general.

Authenticity in Community

Who we are is complicated by how much of us is hidden, denied, or sublimated. Wholeness is a theme of my writing, especially in *When Half Is Whole,* a book of stories of 11 mixed-ancestry persons. The cover shows a half moon, which I first saw as a symbol of how these people are viewed by others as being "half," when in reality they are whole. But I gradually saw the title and image as a metaphor for human development—we begin our lives whole but gradually become fragmented, and parts of us come into darkness. We become disconnected from parts of ourselves. Yet we still have a "hidden wholeness." Our challenge is to remember, see, and reconnect, to embrace those parts of ourselves, returning to our "original wholeness" and becoming the whole person we are always capable of becoming. By embracing the "dark side" or the shadow of our ambiguous natures, we come to know "the light."

The healing power of going into our darkness is documented by research. While for ages people have proclaimed the healing nature of writing, we now have more scientific evidence of this truth and a knowledge of which kinds of writing are best for which situations.[15] We know that writing about oneself has positive impacts on health, including boosting the immune system, lessening pain, and decreasing medication use. This includes writing about trauma, which is known to have therapeutic effects.[16]

Rather than focusing exclusively on happiness, some in the field of positive psychology are endorsing the importance of finding wholeness by connecting to our dark side. This place includes what we typically regard as negative emotions. Making the unconscious conscious integrates the shadow parts of one's self. A whole or authentic person acts in service of what they value, which requires drawing on the full range of psychological states to respond effectively to what life offers.[17]

Heartfulness is created when we bring our authentic selves to *all* our human encounters. We find that when we can be ourselves, it frees others to be *themselves.* We cross borders between ourselves and others. If we can risk vulnerability, be open, and be willing to let others see us for everything we are, we can connect to others without masks. Modeling authentic living in the moment encourages others to consider how to live and how to express themselves from a similar place of authenticity.

If I can bring myself to a situation or an experience as a "whole person," others can bring themselves as whole persons, too. A Stanford student once told me that he rarely went to his other classes, but when he saw how I was bringing myself as completely as possible to the class I was teaching, he felt that he had to do the same, and so he attended every class of mine. Colleagues often warn me that by bringing myself into the classroom I am opening Pandora's box. They fear that I am subjecting myself to psychoanalysis by the students. "Better to leave yourself at the door," they tell me. But I simply can't.

We are all accustomed to bringing a different self to the public, presenting ourselves to others as a performance in which we show a certain socially acceptable and desirable side while we hide other, less-acceptable parts. We are dominated by our ego, with its fears and demands. Freeing ourselves from this prison is hard work. Just being who you really are at any moment is a great challenge. It requires courage to be the real you, relating honestly with others. Authenticity is knowing who are you, and being that person in your daily life, awake and aware of your thoughts and feelings. Through heartfulness we become authentic one moment at a time in our thoughts, feelings, and actions. Many spiritual teachings encourage us to be mindful, listen, and act from the heart, starting from right where we are.

Authenticity means aligning your words with your actions and practicing what you believe and preach, without concern for what others may think of you. When we are authentic we are being real, not phony or masking who we really are, comfortable in our own skin. Being authentic is being genuine and sincere—free from falseness, pretense, or hypocrisy.

After many years as a professional counselor, I know that people find it helpful to be with a person who models openness and self-disclosure. Carl Rogers, the humanistic psychologist, believed that for persons to grow, they need an environment that provides them with genuineness, acceptance, and empathy—one that enables others to also become more open and authentic.

What if we can bring our whole self to parenting, as well? There was a song in my younger days that spoke to authenticity and parenting. The first verse, "Teach your children well," is an expected message to parents, but it's followed by a verse that goes, "Teach your parents well."[18] The message to me is that parenting is a two-way street, *if* we're open to learning from our children.

In my occasional role of speaker to large groups, I see that authenticity even communicates on a big stage. I recently spoke to an assembly of an entire high school of nearly 1,000 students, on "finding meaning in life's struggles." There had been several deaths there, including suicides, and I was asked to convey a healing message. As I prepared my remarks, I reminded myself that I simply needed to be authentic, telling the students only what I know—no more and no less. I silently repeated to myself over and over, "It's all about me," mocking the voice of my own pride and ego, which were of no importance compared to the possible goodness that might be done by spreading a message of loving-kindness. It was my way of accepting that the best I could do for my audience was to be a vessel through which a greater power might transmit wisdom to others, offering myself in service.

What happened in that assembly was truly amazing. I lost all sense of self-absorption, fear of embarrassment or shame, and the desire to impress, and became one with the audience. The psychologist Mihaly Csikszentmihalyi calls it "flow"—the mental state in which a person performing an activity is fully immersed in a feeling of energized focus, full involvement, and enjoyment in the process of the activity.[19] In Zen it is the state of being completely in the moment, focusing on a single task, and finding a sense of calm and happiness in what you are doing. The students felt it, too, and sat there listening deeply. I was told that when I finished they jumped to their feet and applauded warmly. The principal rushed up and gushed, "You hit a home run!"

This reception gave me a wonderful feeling, because I realized that something amazing can happen simply when we are being mindful, vulnerable, and authentic. When we bring ourselves to a situation authentically, we create community as a deeply human encounter. Others in the encounter feel connected, moved, feeling that we say what they feel, express what they suppress, bring out what they keep inside, say who we are—all the while recognizing our mutual human condition. Authenticity cultivates heartfulness by helping us to move beyond simply being mindful, to connecting compassionately with others. It empowers us with a sense of service and responsible action.

EXERCISES

I. Who Am I?

Asking ourselves the simple question "Who am I?" can be both frustrating and revealing. Our response can show us how hard it is to answer this question, and also can reveal who we really believe we are.

1. Ask yourself this question and write down everything that comes to mind.
2. Try not to think about it, and write quickly.
3. After 5 minutes look at your list and reflect on it. Does it show you who you really are? Do you see things about yourself that you would like to develop?

II. What Makes You Feel Alive?

Reminding ourselves of when we feel most alive can bring us closer to realizing who we are and what we want to do, or feel called to do, with our lives.

1. Reflect on this question and write down whatever comes to mind, without censoring, for 10 minutes: "What is my purpose in this world?"
2. Reflect on this question and write down whatever comes to mind, without censoring, for 10 minutes: "What do I care about so much that I would pay to do it?"
3. Look at what you have written and ask yourself what actions you can take to fulfill your purpose to do what you most deeply care about.

4
CONNECTEDNESS

For the white person who wants to know how to be my friend
The first thing you do is to forget that i'm Black.
Second, you must never forget that i'm Black.[1]

—PAT PARKER

The boy in my high school yearbook photo is dressed in a summer kimono, a matching headband tied around his forehead, eyes closed, arms folded, sitting serenely with his back to a blazing fireplace. It was my choice of how I wanted to be photographed and seen by others. The white boys in my school saw me as "almost black," because they had some idea of what it meant to be black, and no idea of what it might mean to be Japanese. Neither did I, but I imagined myself as a cool, tough, calm samurai, as that was the only good image I had, thanks to glorious stories from childhood about my great-grandfather.

The photo caption read: "He represents an easy balance between East and West." Those were not my choice of words. I felt nothing *like* an easy balance. I was off center, romantically searching for understanding who I was and where I belonged. The two seemed inseparable, yet vital to finding my place in the human family. In what would prove to be a tortuous, twisting path, a never-ending journey, I was on my way home.

Connecting with others has always been a challenge for me. Many people have told me that I didn't belong, or *did* belong. Some white kids told me that I didn't belong. Some black kids told me that I *did* belong. When I decided to return to Japan, my American family and some well-intentioned friends questioned my claims of authenticity, insisting that I was really just like them, certainly not Japanese. They pointed out the obvious: I had spent most of my life in the United States surrounded by an Irish family who treasured me, I spoke English better than Japanese, and was American, not Japanese. I ignored them but also asked myself, Why did I need to choose such an extreme path? Why couldn't I be more like my sisters, who adjusted well to their American environment? What impelled me to insist that I was Japanese and return to live in Japan?

Perhaps I was simply seeking to escape from the isolated and alienated world I inhabited by connecting to certain others. The desire for interpersonal union is our most powerful, fundamental passion that keeps the human race together, in the clan, the family, and in society. Our awareness of our disunited existence is an unbearable prison.[2] We liberate ourselves from this prison by uniting ourselves in some form or other with humans, and with the world outside.

Today we have scientific evidence supporting the health benefits of connectedness, as our social networks of friends and family and the strength of our bonds with them are major factors in determining our well-being.[3] People change in connection with others. In contrast to the message of individualistic culture, which typically puts the burden on the individual to initiate and accomplish change, we need to reach outside ourselves and build our network of connections that will nourish and sustain us as we change. This includes family, friends, and community, and possibly a connection with one's own soul, too, as a source of meaning and purpose in our life.

In the previous chapter, we found that a sense of authenticity depends on who we think we are in relation to others. The answer for those who see themselves as autonomous individuals is easier and simpler, but it does not immediately solve their need for connectedness. The answer for those who see themselves as an integral part of something greater is harder, seemingly impossible to distinguish from the related questions: What am I part of? Where do I belong? Where is my community? Who are my people?

My personal experiences told me more about where I didn't belong rather than where I *did* belong. As I grew up I realized I felt not only different but also isolated, even alienated from those around me—a stranger, a marginal man. I wanted to leave my home town to get away from "them," the people with whom I didn't feel connected.

Uniting ourselves with other humans is necessary. The question we face is: With which people do we connect? This depends on with whom we attempt to bond, whom we reject, who includes us, who excludes us. In some of this there is choice, but much is beyond our control. We can escape from the prison of aloneness by aligning with humanity in general or by bonding with a certain group. We can't always see it, but we can also bond with both. My choice was to bond with those whom I perceived to be most like me. It was not the whites or the blacks or the Chinese; for me, it was the Japanese. But the reality is that I had no idea who they were or who I was in relation to them. Once I lived among them, it didn't take long to find out who they thought I was; it took longer for them to see who I *really* was. It took me even longer to realize who I was in relation to them.

Although I noticed how Japanese I was, other aspects of who I was were apparent to those around me, and these aspects gradually, sometimes grudgingly, became apparent to me. I was American, I was Irish, and I was mixed. It took me a while to realize that none of this negated that I was Japanese. This was a great discovery and awakening. I was and had always been Japanese, regardless of what else I was. Over the years I learned to live in many worlds, despite the persistent attempts of others to confine me to the standards of their dichotomous world that told them I must be either this or that. I became more whole, more connected, more the person I was born to be.

Connecting to Self and Other

The process of becoming more whole or more authentic involves connecting to parts of ourselves from which we have become disconnected. Mindfulness, vulnerability, and authenticity, as shown in the previous chapters, are ways we enhance self-awareness, enabling us to become more connected to ourselves. Remembering who we are is experienced as a return to who we were or were meant to be; becoming a whole person may be experienced as a homecoming, as if we are returning home, in peace. In the words of T.S. Eliot:

> *We shall not cease from exploration*
> *And the end of all our exploring*
> *Will be to arrive where we started*
> *And know the place for the first time.*[4]

The great attraction of mindfulness is its promise of personal gain and stress reduction. People imagine that it is an individualistic activity, removing us from the world, practicing on our own, eyes closed, out of contact with those around us. When we practice we realize the effects of mindfulness beyond our internal world, as it enhances our awareness and connection with others.

While mindfulness helps to connect us to ourselves, enhancing self-awareness, it also makes us more aware of and attuned to others, as if we are seeing them clearly for the first time. It is an extraordinarily beautiful moment—two people meeting in joy, trying neither to compete nor to obtain a favor nor to prove a point. Research shows that practitioners of mindfulness can use the awareness they've been cultivating to relate more empathically and kindly with others.[5] This is how connecting with others cultivates heartfulness by extending self-awareness to awareness of others.

Being authentic—accepting all of who we are—empowers us to see our connections with others. Acceptance of others is ultimately about self-understanding. We learn to accept others by realizing our own disturbing "otherness," recognizing it not simply as something that exists on the outside but as something that also exists within.[6] If we are aware of it inside us, we realize the ways in which we are connected with other people. We widen our circle of compassion, including more and more people, other creatures, even the universe.

Einstein reminds us how our existence depends on our connectedness in not merely a mundane sense but in a deeper way, a way in which we can escape from the prison of separateness:

> A human being is a part of the whole called by us universe, a part limited in time and space. He experiences himself, his thoughts and feelings as something separated from the rest—a kind of optical delusion of his consciousness. This delusion is a kind of prison for us, restricting us to our personal desires and to affection for a few persons nearest to us. Our task must be to free ourselves from this

prison by widening our circle of compassion to embrace all living creatures and the whole of nature in its beauty.[7]

The challenge we have as humans is to expand our abilities to develop bonds with many others. As I mature, I feel a growing awareness of what Einstein called the prison of our delusion of separateness. Escape from this prison comes by realizing how we are intimately connected to all other living beings. Feeling connected is necessary for me to be alive, knowing that I am not alone. I know that I am alive when I am compassionate, when I connect with others. Widening the circles of compassion is an ongoing struggle, an integral element of heartfulness.

Respect

Common sense, spiritual teachings, and psychology research all reinforce the belief that it is good to be connected. Our ability to connect with others depends on many things developing from early in life and proceeding through several key stages.

In infancy we need to build trust and attachment. In young adulthood we have to establish lasting and meaningful relationships that develop a sense of bonding and intimacy with others. But because of our fear of rejection or excessive self-preoccupation, we may be unable to form close, meaningful relationships and thus become psychologically isolated, failing to connect with others.

We face the human dilemma that we are complex: part of humanity; part of certain groups; and also unique. All three identities both sustain and threaten us. A group identity poses the threat of nationalism and fundamentalism; individualism threatens us with isolation and alienation. We need global identity to survive, but even that poses a danger if we try to escape from the dangers of groupism and individualism by retreating to a place where we might claim to not see differences.

Asserting that we are more human than anything else need not be a denial of diversity, but often is. Some people claim not to see race or sex, which is impossible for humans, as we naturally see differences and are all socialized to attach values and assumptions to such visible differences. Rather than experiencing "color blindness," we can see differences and acknowledge that these differences may have great meaning in another person's life experiences, and certainly in our own. To deny this reality is to disrespect the person. Rather than either/or, we need to balance both realities.

The beginning of the poem that starts this chapter, "For the white person who wants to know how to be my friend," expresses this need for dual consciousness:

The first thing you do is to forget that i'm Black.
Second, you must never forget that i'm Black.[8]

The way of heartfulness is acknowledging that the black person is indeed black. Respect is seeing a person in his or her complexity—connecting by understanding both similarities and differences. By "seeing" each other completely and clearly, we form the foundation of community that can support the diversity of people and their ways of being.

The Latin origin of the word *respicere* means "to see." To me this means that seeing someone as they are, not how we would like them to be, is respecting that person. Genuine respect is different from the fear and awe we give to authorities and is incompatible with domination and exploitation. If we love the other person, we feel at one with them as they are, not as we need them to be as an object for our use.

We can learn the basic principle of seeing by absorbing the greetings of many cultures. *Namaste* is a Hindi greeting that expresses that "the divine in me recognizes the divine in you." The Zulu word *sawubona* similarly means "I see you," with the response meaning "I am here," an exchange with the deep meaning that, by the act of being seen by you, I have come into existence. The Hebrew word *hineni* also has this profound meaning of "here I am," in the sense that I am here for you.

The writing of feminist scholar Gloria Anzaldua shows a heartful way of seeing our goal as neither glossing over differences nor using them to separate us from others. Many of us in contemporary society identify with groups and social positions not limited to our ethnic, racial, religious, class, gender, or national classifications; we define who we are by what we include instead of by what we exclude. Anzaldua urges us all to become more comfortable with those who step over the line, with hybridities and ambiguities, with what does not fit our expectations of race and sex. She defines "spiritual activism" as a way of thinking and being in which we move beyond separate and easy identifications, creating bridges that cross race and other classifications among different groups:

> Staying home and not venturing out from our own group comes from woundedness, and stagnates our growth. To bridge means loosening our borders, not closing off to others. Bridging is the work of opening the gate to the stranger,

within and without. To step across the threshold is to be stripped of the illusion of safety because it moves us into unfamiliar territory and does not grant safe passage. To bridge is to attempt community, and for that we must risk being open to personal, political, and spiritual intimacy, to risk being wounded. Effective bridging comes from knowing when to close ranks to those outside our home, group, community, nation—and when to keep the gates open.[9]

In heartful communities, we create empathy and respect by seeing others clearly. We create bridges with two-way traffic, each person crossing over to the other side. We do away with separations like "ours" and "theirs," instead honoring and embracing people's differences in a vulnerable way. We open ourselves to be changed rather than punishing others for having a different view, belief system, skin color, or spiritual practice. When people bring a diversity of perspectives, it alters and expands the dialogue in a synergistic manner.

Anzaldua explains the beauty of the Spanish word *nosotros* in crossing this divide. Combining "us" and "others" into one word signifies our unity, questioning and altering the age-old binary of "us vs. them."

Heartfulness begins with the personal and then moves outward, acknowledging our interconnectedness. This counters the tendencies for our goals to become merely those of acquiring materialistic items and enhancing our personal well-being, when the focus is on the individual. In heartful communities, respect is shown by recognizing differences among us, yet insisting on our commonalities. We try to let go of specific categories of identity, while recognizing that they may still be necessary at times. We recognize the need for an alternative vision, a beloved community where being connected to the other is seen as the foundation of a healthy self, and where the "other" is seen as a part of us.[10]

Crossing Borders

In Nelson Mandela, the beloved South African leader, we see a life of heartfulness, characterized by transformative learning, social responsibility, and expanding consciousness of connectedness. Mandela started from being part of a small village and tribe, but in college he made friends with a man from a different tribe and began to lose the grip of the tribalism that imprisoned him. From there, he began to sense his identity as African. When he moved to a larger university, his circle of friends widened even further. His activity in student politics convinced him to build coalitions with students of various loyalties, giving him pride in pan-African culture as well as a larger source of identity. He later made his first friendship with a white man, and the experience of becoming part of a group of people who did not seem to pay any attention to color at all was both frightening and exhilarating. Mandela's story is of a persistently widening sense of self that matured into his extraordinary commitment to include all South Africans in a common future:

> I was beginning to see that my duty was to my people as a whole, not just a particular section or branch. I felt that all the currents of my life were taking me away from my tribe toward what seemed like the center, a place where regional and ethnic loyalties gave way before a common purpose."[11]

Later, in prison, the kindness Mandela received from an officer and the affection he felt toward a guard were experiences that reinforced his belief in the essential humanity of even those who would keep us behind bars. It is this conviction of the essential humanity of the other that turns "us" and "them" into a shared "we," making it possible for us to work together for the common good.

This kind of border crossing occurred in my own family when my father and mother came together following a tragic war in which they had been on opposite sides. They overcame that radical division and transcended the barriers of countries, religions, and races, affirming that love crosses borders constructed by humans. My Japanese grandparents accepted my American father, and then their mixed-race grandchildren, into their home in the understanding that we are all connected. My Irish family also accepted us as kin (though they did require us to become Catholic).

Holding onto labels is destructive—erecting walls that separate us from each other. We each have our own way of dividing the world into "us" and "them." This is a dehumanizing process that leads to fear and violence. When I was young, I saw people in the military as bad and destructive. But when I later accepted an offer from the U.S. Marines to provide diversity and leadership training, I learned how "they" were simply human beings like me. "They" had a different idea about how to survive and help others. I did not agree with their way but I tried to understand it and empathize with them. I saw that I, too, had similar feelings or thoughts that might lead me to try to resolve problems by force. We—they *and* I—were more similar than I had thought. And I was part of the problem;

they were "my" military since I was a tax-paying citizen. While maintaining my own beliefs, I practiced deep listening, trying to understand why they thought the way they did, coming to a much deeper place of understanding both self and other.

In her later writings, Gloria Anzaldua called for shifting our focus from what has been done to us, to what we're doing to each other, to those in distant countries, and even to the Earth's environment. She notes that we are motivated to act collaboratively with the knowledge that we live in symbiotic relationship to all that exists, as cocreators of ideologies—attitudes, beliefs, and cultural values.[12] She reminds us that living in multicultural communities demands that we develop a perspective that takes into account the entire planet.

In heartful communities we address a major barrier to connectedness: our sense of victimization. It enables us to connect to certain people yet separates us from still others. Sharing personal and cultural stories becomes a way for us to cross borders, to see new connections with those who we thought were different from us. We discover that some of us have visible differences or wounds, while in others these lie hidden.

In these communities, we come to realize that we are not alone in our struggles but are connected and interdependent. We are concerned for what is happening in our neighborhoods, whether they be south of the border or far across the sea. I see my students, who are divided in many ways—by sex, race, class, or gender—go through this process. They observe the differences between themselves and certain others at first, but gradually they begin to notice their similarities. Making these connections where they imagined none existed is exhilarating and liberates them from the prison of aloneness. The recognition of our connectedness gives us compassion for what is affecting our sisters and brothers anywhere in the world. In heartfulness we all rise or sink together.

Empathy

In my work of designing heartful spaces, I try to help others seek connectedness through empathy—a key concept in many fields. Design thinkers are taught to empathize with their clients to understand who they are and what is important to them. Gaining clues about what they think, feel, and need will lead to insights that give them the direction to create innovative solutions. The best solutions come out of the best insights into human behavior.

The kind of empathy being called on is referred to by some psychologists as cognitive empathy.[13] Others call it perspective taking, and it simply consists of knowing how the other person feels and imagining what they might be thinking. This is helpful in product design, negotiations, and motivating people, among many other activities. But the limitation to cognitive empathy is that some people can be talented in this regard while having no real concern for others. Cognitive empathy alone is often insufficient to create genuine connectedness.

In heartful work, we are looking for deeper forms of empathy. Emotional empathy means being moved by a connection with another. Social neuroscience tells us this kind of empathy may depend on the mirror neuron system. The connection created between people is useful in all kinds of human relations—at work, at play, with friends and family. But it can also be negative, if the emotions exhaust or detach the person in burnout. This may lead to indifference instead of caring.

The goal of heartful communities is to express compassionate empathy. With this kind of empathy, we understand a person's difficulty and feel with them. We are also spontaneously moved to help, if needed, so empathy may be a step toward compassion.

Brain science reveals that mindfulness may increase our ability to be helpful. When experienced meditators encounter suffering in another person, the meditators' brains show heightened activity in areas that are important in activities such as caring, nurturing, and establishing positive social affiliation. In nonmeditators, the same stimuli trigger the brain areas associated with unpleasant feelings of sadness and pain. Some psychologists call the caring response compassion and the latter empathy.

Heartfulness is a way of expressing compassion, or compassionate empathy, rather than cognitive and emotional forms of empathy. Compassion is connected to responsibility. In the words of Dag Hammarskjold, the second Secretary-General of the United Nations and a posthumous recipient of the Nobel Peace Prize, *"In our age, the road to holiness necessarily passes through the world of action."*[14] Heartfulness focuses our energies on doing what we can in service. We learn how to be compassionate rather than empathic to address problems such as depression, burnout, and narcissism. With more wisdom and less fear, we become a loving force in the world.

Fear often acts as a barrier to empathy and compassion. We see this increasingly in diverse communities where we encounter people whose customs, food, and clothes, as well as attitudes to sexuality, time, work, money, manners, and sense of duty, differ from ours. The initial reaction to them is often suspicion or fear; prejudice has deep roots.

In heartful communities, we begin crossing borders with mindfulness, leading to a greater willingness to be vulnerable and authentic. Seeing and listening, we realize connectedness. This enhances our ability to understand the experience of others. In encountering others, we are given the opportunity to learn valuable lessons not only about them but also about ourselves. In these relationships of co-constructed reality, people work together to find new meaning and new ways of being.

Heartfulness is grounded in the reality that we are more alike than different, more human than anything else. A basic recognition that humans share concerns about living and dying must underlie the relationship that we hope to establish with any person. Empathy depends on feeling this common ground and common bond, regardless of apparent differences.

Emphasizing our human commonalties is a warm invitation to dialogue and share differences; this is far better than inducing alienating and divisive feelings by overemphasizing our differences. An understanding of our shared humanity—that we are like all other humans—is essential to both empathy and compassion.

Heartful communities are based in connected knowing, an approach in which we look for strengths, not weaknesses, in another's argument.[15] If a weakness is perceived, we struggle to understand why someone might think that way. The more we disagree with another person, the harder we try to understand how that person could imagine such a thing, using empathy, imagination, and storytelling as tools for entering into the other person's frame of mind. We try to enter into their perspective, adopting their frame of mind, seeing the world through their eyes.

Since we show empathy and true respect, the other person may find their voice or feel appreciated for contributing their ideas.[16] We encourage listening with the heart, offering genuineness, and learning each other's stories, visions, and goals. A high degree of collaboration results, and creativity springs forth.

Our movement is like aikido applied to human relations. Aikido was developed by Morihei Ueshiba as a martial arts philosophy of extending love and compassion especially to those who seek to harm others. This is done by developing the ability to receive an attack and harmlessly redirect it. Aikido works by connecting with the other, a "way of combining forces," blending with an attacker's movements for the purpose of controlling their actions with minimal effort. In an ideal resolution, the receiver is unharmed, and so is the attacker. In human relations, this is a "win-win" solution.

Our heartfulness approach is like Goethe's "gentle empiricism," as we are trying to enter into the other person's perspective, adopting their frame of mind, trying to see the world through their eyes. We are striving to get the big picture, trying to see things holistically, not analytically. We see and feel with the other, trying to receive the other into ourselves. This creates a situation that can work for everyone—creating a level playing field where even very dissimilar people can meet as equals. This is especially important in multicultural groups, as certain cultural rules will make some members more competent than others in participating. Practices of connected knowing empower marginalized, silenced, less formally educated members, enabling them to contribute to the group.

In empathy, we find points of connection in our diverse experiences. Author Hirotada Ototake expressed this well in a dialogue with Ariana Miyamoto, the offspring of a Japanese mother and an African-American father, who was the controversial Japan representative in the 2015 Miss Universe contest.[17] Ototake said:

> You and I are highly visible minorities—me with no arms or legs, and you with dark skin. But in this country I think that many people who are not visible minorities find it a hard place to

live. Among those who appear to be "majority people" are many who suffer from feelings of being different and suppressing their true selves. I hope it becomes a society where people can live more freely and openly, with individuality recognized and accepted. For these people who feel the pain of not being able to reveal their real identities and are living by hiding their authenticity, I think it's important for visible minorities like you and me to raise our voices.

Ototake draws the connections between his experience as a person without arms and legs and Miyamoto's experience as a dark-skinned person. He then widens the circle by identifying with all those who feel different and constrained both by their feelings of difference and by their need to hide it. In heartful communities, we draw connections between those with diverse forms of visible differences, and then we include those whose feelings of difference are invisible, thereby widening our circle of inclusion. We create space for vulnerability and authenticity, creating a sense of community. Feeling that they are in a safe place, members conquer their fears and open themselves to others by sharing intimate stories, and are often amazed to find that the borders between them can be crossed in realizing their interconnectedness. As one student of mine wrote:

> One thing that I particularly will be taking away from this class is an appreciation for how connected we all are. It amazed me how even though I was discussing class topics with people who I didn't know very well, I still managed to at least sympathize with what they were saying, if not completely agree and understand. So many of us have gone through similar situations in life and had the same struggles, it just amazes me how there is such a potential for connection that is totally lost in the concept of the stranger. It makes me more willing to reach out and meet new people. The biggest lesson I can take here is that other people are not dangerous or scary, and that most of them are not trying to hurt me,

but heal me and themselves, even if they don't know it.

Oneness

My sense of connectedness was unwittingly nourished early in life by my father, who wailed incessantly about the incredible suffering he saw in the world. He confessed that it destroyed his faith both in his fellow humans and in a benevolent God. It also drove him to drink, and left him hopeless about creating a kind and just world. Witnessing suffering made him dismissive of happiness as a state of mind possible only to a person who denied and neither saw nor felt the horrors of this world. He claimed that he could not be happy if there was someone, somewhere, who was suffering.

I saw that he was sincere when he shocked me, one lazy summer afternoon. We were at the beach, sitting on a blanket watching children playing in the water, when my father startled me by saying, "I hope that I never see a child drowning ... because I would have to go in to try to save him, even though I know it would kill me." My father had a bad heart that had been surgically repaired. It surprised me that he knew that if he saw a child drowning he would try to save him, even though he would die in the process.

I couldn't understand how he could even *think* of doing that. Where would that leave me? I wouldn't have a dad anymore. So I asked him, "Why would you *do* that, Daddy?" His answer was, "I couldn't just sit here and watch a kid die; I wouldn't be able to live with myself."

This story remains with me today as a testament to compassionate empathy—an immediate connection you might form with another person, to the degree that you forget yourself and your safety and spontaneously do what is necessary. While Dad's inability to act would be called emotional empathy, his potential for heroic action is compassionate empathy. Despite our separation from individuals, we have an amazing need to connect and a capacity for immediate empathy that transcends those we're close to. In the midst of a catastrophe—when someone's life is in danger—we may suddenly throw ourselves into the situation to take care of them, as if they were our own souls. We see this all the time in response to natural disasters or crises.

The hero is one who has given his physical life to that truth. But whether you love your neighbor or not, when the realization grabs you, you may risk your life. In such a psychological crisis you suddenly realize, without thinking, that you and the other are one—that you are two aspects of a single life. Our apparent separateness is but an effect of the way we experience forms under the conditions of space and time. We are conscious of our separateness, while our true reality lies in our unity with *all* life. This is a truth that may become spontaneously realized under circumstances of crisis, which tend to connect us with others.

In small ways, you can see this happening every day, all the time—people doing selfless things to and for each other. In our daily lives we have a strong need to connect with others, to overcome our separateness, to leave the confinement of our aloneness. The growing science of empathy provides evidence that we are wired for compassion, but nevertheless there remains something mysterious about our need for deep connectedness. We may consider this mystery as religion, spirituality, philosophy, or perhaps simply healing.

In heartful communities, empathy, compassion, and love are central to our approach of how we relate to the world as a whole, not toward a single object of love. The truth of oneness is an active power that breaks through the walls that separate us from our fellow women and men. We unite with others, which lets us overcome the sense of isolation and separateness. This is the highest form of connectedness with others and with the world.

Heartfulness honors the call expressed at the beginning of this chapter: to first see the other as fundamentally the same human being as ourself. We also acknowledge the differences between us, knowing that they can tremendously affect the life experiences of both of us. We connect in the respect given in seeing the other person in their wholeness, uniting with them in mindful compassion.

EXERCISES

I. First Impressions

We often limit our relationships by assuming differences, when similarities also exist between ourselves and people we meet.

1. Reflect on someone you know well, but didn't think you would become friends with when you first met.
2. Remember what made you distant from this person at first.
3. Notice what happened as you got to know the person.
4. Write about this reflection for at least 10 minutes.

II. Finding Connections

Finding things that we have in common with another person may arouse empathy. Seeing how we are similar can help us to realize our connections, thereby overcoming our fear of differences.

1. Think of either someone whom you know well or someone you

know just a little. Focusing on a person whom you don't like may be helpful.
2. Think of the things you have in common with that person—the ways in which you share some characteristic or experience—and then write them down.
3. Read the list.
4. Close your eyes, take a deep breath, and bring the person to your mind, noticing how you feel about them now.

5

LISTENING

The most precious gift we can offer others is our presence. When mindfulness embraces those we love, they will bloom like flowers. The miracle is not to walk on water. The miracle is to walk on the green earth, dwelling deep in the present moment and feeling fully alive.[1]
—THICH NHAT HANH

When I was told that I had been assigned a person named Yoshiko Meyers to visit, the questions began. What do you talk about with someone who is dying? Would they be interested in small talk about the weather outside their room? Does the news hold any importance for them? Would they like to talk about their religious beliefs? But what if they have none? Would they want to talk about their feelings?

And if they wanted to talk about death, what could I possibly say?

I was a hospice volunteer in Boston, a young man on my way to graduate school with the goal of becoming a psychologist. I thought that I was supposed to talk with Yoshiko about dying, and while I reassured myself that I was ready, I knew that I was not. I had been assigned to her because of our shared cultural backgrounds. I tried to understand what it meant to be Japanese and facing death. My grandmother talked openly about dying, mostly about acceptance, saying *shikata ga nai,* it can't be helped, we all have to die. She also spoke of her desire to avoid *meiwaku,* burdening the family. I thought that I should ask Yoshiko how she felt about dying, but never found the right moment.

From my understanding of *Bushido*, accepting that death is inevitable and certain brings an appreciation of life, an openness to life as it is, in each moment. I comforted myself with the belief that since death came to everyone, there was no reason to fear it. I sensed that the fear of death and the desire for life are intricately intertwined, thus the denial of death leads to a numbing of the life force as well. Unlike people who reach this realization after their own confrontation with death through a serious illness or a near-death experience, I needed to find another way. Perhaps that is why I was drawn to hospice—I was striving to overcome my fear of death by believing what I was learning from Shunryu Suzuki's teaching about oneness:

> When you do not realize that you are one with the river, or one with the universe, you have fear. Whether it is separated into drops or not, water is water. Our life and

death are the same thing. When we realize this fact, we have no fear of death any more and we have no difficulty in our life.[2]

I began to sense that my fear came from placing Yoshiko in a special category as a dying person, separate and distant. I felt that those like myself, not dying, were distinct from those like Yoshiko, who *were* dying. This feeling of separateness reinforced the fear of death. I sensed that the way of overcoming this separateness was to see that Yoshiko was not special. Like her, I too was dying. It helped to realize that I am confronted with the problem just as much as she, blocked by my identification with my body and mind as my whole being.[3]

I wondered what I could do during my time with Yoshiko. I sensed that to care is to become one with another, to join with a person beyond the cultural, racial, gender, and all other barriers we erect between ourselves and others. I saw that the opportunity to be with Yoshiko was a means of working on myself, and that I would be effective only if I was affected.

I should have known all along that I was not there to counsel or to teach, but to learn. As I sat with her I slowly began to realize that I did not have to do anything. I just needed to be willing to be there, as present as possible without withdrawing. I was not there to save her. I could do nothing to relieve her suffering, but at least I should not run from it. I had to avoid the desire to alleviate her discomfort as a means of alleviating my own. Whatever she was experiencing, I wanted to have room in my heart for receiving it. I realized that this was a matter of the heart, not the head. I struggled to open my heart to her, fighting my impulse to pull away rather than enter the fire.

Yoshiko drifted in and out of consciousness. Her breath was like the sound of waves in the quiet apartment. I could see the gentle rise and fall of her chest beneath the blanket. Unconsciously, I began to breathe with her. The only sound was that of our shared breath. I felt a strange sense of unity, as though we were somehow joined in the mystery and wonder.

Was this mystical feeling a sign that we are all connected far beyond the limits of our ordinary consciousness? Was caring the way that we reach beyond the illusion of separateness that traps us in our bodies and minds? Were we simply two parts of the same whole? If we believe that there is no other, then there is just being, experienced from different focal points. I sensed that if I could be fully present, there would be no such thing as another person, just two perceptions of the same existence.

We never did talk much. I don't know what I provided for her, but I do know what I received. Perhaps sensing my discomfort, Yoshiko was compassionate—knowing that I was sitting next to her because I wanted to help, and wanted to learn. I simply believed that it was important to cherish life until the very end. And that is why I was sitting there by the bed of this stranger—in the hope that whatever growth could take place in her last moments might somehow be assisted by my mere presence.

One night I drifted off to sleep as I sat there. When I awoke and glanced over at her, I found Yoshiko gazing deeply into my eyes with a look that expressed to me her gratitude for my presence. Her eyes communicated a tenderness and kindness that I associate with images of a compassionate Buddha or Christ. I felt a powerful sensation that she was possibly telling me that she was on her way out of this world, and reassuring me that everything would be all right.

The next day I received a phone call from the nurse, telling me that Yoshiko had died. When I hung up I cried for this person who had once been a stranger and yet had entered so deeply into my life. I cried for myself, too, for I knew in that moment that I shared her fate.

It was not clear to me at the time, but I was searching for knowledge of life through confrontation with death. And although I found it hard to know what to say to Yoshiko, it may be that very few people can respond on a verbal level to any concepts about dying. To try to convey seemingly profound messages may only bring on confusion or an intellectual discussion. Without words, I believed I was saying to her, "I know that you suffer," and "I am here for you." I sensed that offering her my true presence was the best I could do.

I had learned to just sit by Yoshiko's bed and wait, trying to be present to what was happening, with a spirit of willingness to help. I had listened with my heart to what she was experiencing or saying. I could only be open and hopefully enter a space of surrender, acceptance, or oneness, in which it may be easier for the dying one to embrace the mystery and wonder.

The Heart of Listening

I was sitting with Yoshiko because I had learned that listening was a way to experience the beauty and wonder of being alive that is heartfulness. I was there at her bedside in a state of mindfulness, simply being present with her, often silent. I felt compassion, not escaping from the reality of her situation, and suffering with her. And I was there with a feeling of responsibility, with the desire to respond to her needs to the best of my ability.

From childhood I had sensed that listening had value and that words were neither always necessary nor sufficient. Listening was done with the heart. My father made it clear that he wanted, perhaps needed, me to be by his side when he had stories to tell. His stories required a listener. That became my role with him. I learned that people could connect through stories and that listening was a gift to be given. Dad never seemed to need me to say much; he just wanted me to *be* there, really listening. Although I sometimes thought I should be saying something, I kept him company and sensed that maybe that was good enough.

My father delighted in telling stories that were imbued with important life lessons. Though I didn't always understand them, the stories planted seeds, some of which later sprouted as life experiences where their meaning came forth. My mother's stories, by contrast, were mostly without words. She told her stories with her way of being and doing. Few words were needed; the message was clear.

When I first started to work as a teenager, my summer jobs in hospitals and nursing homes brought me in contact with people, some silent, but many wanting to tell their stories. I seemed to know how to listen, and while I washed them or was wheeling them around, I'd ask them questions and they'd talk. I learned a lot about their lives. Some would reminisce; others would complain about the pain, or rage about how life was cruel and unfair. "Why me?" they'd ask, knowing I had no answer. Some even shocked me by confiding that they were tired of life, didn't want to be a burden, and really wanted to die. I just listened. I didn't know what to say, but they didn't seem to mind.

The depth and profundity of that role only gradually became clear to me. I realized that they appreciated that I listened to them, acknowledging them and their pain. One of the great lessons I later learned from offering counseling is the gift we give others by simply being present and listening. This insight has sustained and encouraged me as I attempt to empathize and offer compassionate care. It helps me provide human company rather than trying to solve the person's problems.

I realized that my ability to comprehend and help others soothe their feelings is valuable. I found out that listening to stories could even be considered work and part of a job. Eventually, I was someone to whom others turned in times of greatest emotional need. Following my experience with Yoshiko, I became a counseling psychologist—a professional listener. I learned a lot as I studied with great teachers at Harvard and trained with master counselors at hospitals and schools. I came to understand theories of all kinds and to know my patients and clients through these theories. But the more I studied and practiced, the more it was apparent that the heart of counseling is listening, and listening is a matter of the heart.

The heart of listening is shown clearly in the *kanji* for *kiku,* 聴. There is an ear, which is no surprise, as in listening we use our ears to hear what is being said—not only the words, but also the way something is said, the tone of voice, the flow of speech. *Kiku* also contains the number 10 and an eye, indicating maximal seeing, as listening requires more than just our ears, but also other senses, because so much of communication is nonverbal.

Truly sensitive listening demands that we become aware of several kinds of communication besides verbal. People give messages through silences, gestures, facial expressions, and bodily postures. The way a speaker hesitates in her speech can tell us much about her feelings. So, too, can the inflection of her voice. She may stress certain points loudly and clearly, and may mumble others. We can also note such things as the person's hand or eye movements, or breathing, as all of these help to convey her total message.

More-ancient versions of *kiku* contain the symbol for king, perhaps because he receives reports from his ministers and therefore needs to be a good listener. It also has the number one, showing the importance of focused attention. There is no mouth in *kiku,* showing us that our desire to speak often interferes with our ability to listen. We sometimes talk because we do not feel like listening. But in true listening there is silence. While there is a time to ask the right questions, we need to stop interrupting so that the other person's story can be told.

The heart of *kiku* is what impresses me most—we listen with our hearts. This is the basis of empathy, feeling what the other is feeling, and of compassion, feeling moved to alleviate their suffering. Perhaps our ability to listen works much like the diastolic function of the heart to receive blood in a state of relaxation and expansion. We accept what the person communicates by creating space within ourselves. We may also reach out to them more fully, just as the heart pumps blood to the body. The heart is both an open, receptive dimension of our being and an active, expansive opening to the world.[4]

Reflecting on these multiple aspects of *kiku* helps me to understand how complex true listening really is. It demands overcoming our inner distractions and desires to assess, analyze, interpret, diagnose, and prescribe by concentrating the full power of presence on the other person.

Professional Listening

As a Harvard student, I learned about listening from Kiyo Morimoto, the mentor whom I mentioned previously. His approach to counseling was based on the power of listening. He believed that the most important thing we could do was to be as fully present as possible in each moment with the client. The best we could offer was our human company.

"Listen," he constantly admonished us.

We nodded, "Yes, okay, we're listening. Now what else do we do?"

Kiyo would answer, "You're not listening."

We would assure him that we were. After a few rounds of these kinds of exchanges, we students felt frustrated, expecting more from a Harvard education, yet Kiyo persisted in challenging us.

Kiyo taught that without being seen where we *are,* humans find it hard to move, and no matter how good the advice may be, we defy the determined efforts of others to change us. A battle for power and control ensues in which defenses go up and options seem to disappear, while resistances arise. Creative effort to prevent annihilation bursts forth in a fight for one's very existence.

Some in the helping professions wrestle with a misguided idea that listening is a waste of time. They think that the more they know, the less they need to listen. They are even proud of their "professional" ability to diagnose and treat without needing to truly listen to the patient.

I realized I had strayed from the path when a professor supervising me told me bluntly one day, "You're a worse counselor now than when you came to this program." I was stunned because I was discussing a case in the manner in which I had been taught at the hospital—intellectually, analytically, professionally. But he was telling me that something basic was missing from my presentation. There was no heart in it. When I reflected on this later, I was relieved to realize that he was giving me permission to do what I believe and to trust in the process of listening with the heart.

I learned that we begin our care by listening to the patient's account of what has occurred and confirming our reception of their story. Listening enables us to see their needs and desires and to receive their suffering, realizing that in our hearts we are no different from them, giving rise to compassion. Good listening means to listen for the total meaning, not just the content of the message but also the feeling. Often the content is far less important than the feeling that underlies it, so the listener must try to remain sensitive to the total meaning the message has for the speaker. What is he trying to tell me? What does this mean to him?

Listening with "the ear of the heart," in the words of Saint Benedict, is what enables others to speak. Suffering is often trapped inside without a voice. Behind their fearful silence, people want to find and speak their voices, and to have their voices heard. If we listen to even the unspoken communication, someday the person may speak with truth and confidence. We do this with mindful awareness, making space and honoring the other, by not rushing to fill their silences with fearful speech of our own and not trying to coerce them into saying things we want to hear. If we can enter empathically into their world, we may be perceived as someone who has the promise of being able to hear their truth.

We now have more evidence of what is going on in our brains when we listen empathically. Studies show how neurons that are found in various parts of the brain are activated when we perceive another's emotions, automatically and unconsciously creating that state inside us.[5] We can see that empathy is built into human beings, as our nervous system resonates with the same pattern of neural activity in the other person when we attune fully to their experience.

If we sense that our experiences are similar, we can empathize in a way that promotes a connection soothing to the other person. Emotional understanding of others is directly linked to our awareness and understanding of ourselves. We need to know what we are feeling, though it may not be what the other person is feeling. This kind of listening is nonverbal; no words need be spoken by either person.

Growing into the role of professional counselor helped me realize that listening enables us to touch the core emotional elements that make us human. Engaging in the thoughts of another, understanding, empathizing, and responding to their emotional state frees us of our own insecurities, self-absorption, and isolation. Listening is a most precious gift we can both give and receive that helps us realize our connectedness with others.

The realization that I was giving something to patients by listening to them came before the more humbling awareness of how much I was receiving from them by listening. Reflecting now on my work as a counselor, I am struck by how I am richer from receiving the gift of others' stories. Our encounters are mini-dramas in which patient and caregiver each play teaching roles, passing on stories. If we can listen respectfully, with undivided attention, the stories can be received as gifts. We can be healed by others' stories. In helping others to find hope, we can find hope ourselves. How many times have others tended to me, calmed my fears, and relieved me of guilt with their stories? Although I am the one designated to counsel the sick and troubled, I am faced with someone who is experiencing something I have never known and yet deeply want to know. A voice inside me asks, "How do they *do* it? How do they *live* in such circumstances?" Their stories give me the answers.

Listening cultivates heartfulness if we acknowledge that, to be effective, we must be affected. As the psychiatrist Carl Jung asserted, "only the wounded physician heals."[6] More than anything we do or say, what helps a person who is suffering is who we are—our perspective on life, our love and respect for others, our awareness of our own suffering and the extent to which we have worked through it.

Active Listening

Listening is a matter of the heart but is also something that we can learn through behavioral skills. The role of the listener goes beyond passively hearing what is said. In the 18th century book *Hagakure,* we see how *Bushido* valued the active role of the listener:

> Praise his good points and use every device to encourage him, perhaps by talking about one's own faults without touching on his, but so that they will occur to him. Have him receive this in the way that a man would drink water when his throat is dry, and it will be an opinion that will correct faults.[7]

More recently, the psychologist Carl Rogers introduced the concept of active listening as an important way to witness. Active listening is a way of connecting to the stories that others tell. It requires that we get inside the speaker and grasp, from their point of view, what they are communicating to us. This is empathy. More than merely understanding the other's feelings, we must convey to the speaker that we are seeing things from their point of view:

> By consistently listening to a speaker, you are conveying the idea that: "I'm interested in you as a person, and I think that what you feel is important. I respect your thoughts, and even if I don't agree with them, I know that they are valid for you. I feel sure that you have a contribution to make. I'm not trying to change you or evaluate you. I just want to understand you. I think you're worth listening to, and I want you to know that I'm the kind of a person you can talk to."[8]

These are principles I teach in active listening:
1. Listen for the story—Pay attention to the words being spoken and how they are being said.
2. Listen with all your senses—Notice nonverbal communication

expressed in the person's body language.
3. Listen with your heart—Pay attention to the emotions that the person is projecting and that you are feeling.
4. Acknowledge that you are listening—Verbally and/or nonverbally let the person know you are listening.
5. Reflect back to the person what you are hearing and feeling—Repeat what you are hearing, to help the person clarify their feelings.
6. Invite the person to say more—Ask questions for clarification or further explanation, showing your interest.
7. Be nonjudgmental—Create a sense of safety by suspending your judgment or blame.
8. Temper your curiosity—Try to control your curiosity and questions that lead the person away from their story.
9. Share your feelings—Try to notice positive or hopeful signs in the person, and share those.

After practicing their listening skills, students often remark that listening to others is surprisingly interesting. They realize that if they really listen, everyone has something fascinating to say, even the people who appear most ordinary or boring. Those they had dismissed or distanced as not having anything original, relevant, or interesting to say are, in fact, genuinely real. Even more revelatory is the awareness that through listening they can connect with those who they thought were so "different" that there would be no bridging the gap.

While listening is crucial in health and medical contexts, it is, of course, also important in all human relations. We all know the common experience of not being listened to and how that makes us feel. If we are only partially heard or frequently interrupted or ignored, we stop talking about our experiences or ideas. If we experience this regularly, we begin to feel that no one cares about us, leading to discouragement, depression, or even anger.

Heartfulness emphasizes listening respectfully, feeling the other's anguish, and extending empathy and compassion. We join with others as a whole presence. We find that when we listen with our hearts others tell us more about their lives, mutual trust builds, and healing occurs. We may hear something important that helps us to understand the person's condition better and to take efficacious action on their behalf. Or we may simply bear witness to their suffering, and in so doing help to heal the other's wounds. Listening with the heart may be the best we can offer; at times it may be *all* we have to offer.

We all understand that there are limits on listening—it takes time and energy. We need to take care of our own needs and those of others for whom we are responsible, in our families, communities, and professional work. We sense, too, that endless, repetitive talking about a problem may no longer be doing the person any good. Keeping these real, practical limitations in mind, we can still benefit from a mindful, listening way of being.

Listening in Parenting

Parenting in many cultures is regarded as a one-way transmission of knowledge from parent to child. The child is expected to listen. But my experience tells me that listening is more complex. Even Amy Chua, who was vilified as the Tiger Mom who cruelly forced her style of discipline on her children, admitted, "maybe it all comes down to—listen to your child."[9] This doesn't mean that we have to do what our children want; it simply means that we respect them enough to listen. In this way, we can sense what it is that they really need. When we parent with heartfulness, we encourage ourselves to listen, realizing how much we can learn by paying attention.

Heartful parenting involves not only learning how to listen so that your child will talk, but also talking to your child in a way that they will listen to you. We encourage children to listen when we acknowledge feelings rather than blaming, shaming, or labeling. Kids will listen better if we describe what we see rather than making general statements, and offer options rather than make strict demands or give rigid orders. We enable kids to listen when we make "I" statements that express our feelings, rather than "you" statements that may feel like attacks and therefore arouse defenses.

We may find it especially effective and gratifying when we respond to our child's desires by acknowledging rather than negating. In a typical scenario, one of my sons would ask for a treat before meal time. A natural response would be, "No, you can't have it; it's too close to dinner and it will spoil your appetite." This answer prompts a reaction in the child to push even harder, and the situation escalates and gets out of hand quickly.

But if I responded more empathically, the situation often de-escalated:

"I know you really want it, don't you? It looks so yummy. Me, too; I want one. But if we eat one now we won't be able to eat dinner. Let's have some after dinner!"

Heartful parenting does not have to be verbal. As a child, I was struck by how my Japanese mother communicated without words and expected her children to do the same. Americans are often incredulous when I tell them that my mother never says, "I love you." She never needed to. Her children understood the depth of her love without being told in words. She taught me that this form of shared understanding was subtle, sincere, and beautiful. I learned to be sensitive to others' nonverbal and implicit forms of communication. I grew up associating silence with truthfulness.

Listening in Community

> The wound will not heal until given witness.[10]
> —RUMI

In heartful communities, we acknowledge that the most fundamental thing we can do is to be present for each other. Pauses and silences are encouraged from the very beginning in heartful communities. In my experience, these occur naturally in Japan, a culture in which there is a word, *ma,* that recognizes the meaning of the empty space between words or musical notes. There is comfort and respect in silence. The effort may be to encourage speaking from people who have been silenced through socialization. There are many Americans, as well as some people in other societies, who have been silenced by those in power or by oppressive structures that make them invisible and unheard.

The dominant American culture has socialized students to value speaking over listening. It is a habit for which some have been repeatedly rewarded for mastering. But I tell them to slow down, let go of the need to talk, and instead be mindful, listen, and reflect. "You don't need to say anything," I tell them. "I won't judge you negatively for not talking. I will judge you positively for listening." Practicing mindfulness at the beginning of classes or workshops helps all to respect the silences and to listen.

We live in a world filled with misunderstanding and disputes, where the capacity to communicate is essential. Yet the American educational system favors and rewards the orally assertive, nurturing experts at communicating their ideas to others, by arguing, persuading, convincing, and influencing. We become unable to listen, our minds filled with thoughts about how to present our ideas and how to win arguments. Schools claim to value cooperation and collaboration, while actually encouraging children to think about what to say next and thus to compete with each other. This self-centered focus makes it difficult to listen, making much of what we consider to be communication merely the exchange of rhetoric.

Heartfulness values genuine conversation and dialogue in which speaking and listening both occur in a dance and a kind of play between two human beings. This naturally creates harmony and is an art that benefits both oneself and the other.

The dance of speaking and listening is expressed in story telling. We understand experience by constructing stories and listening to the stories of others. Storytellers remind us of the human need to tell our stories and to have someone listen. This is true in daily life and also in places like health care. Patients are people, each with an "illness narrative" that explains how they became ill and what can be done to heal. The job of the clinician is to listen to that story and make sense of it so that help can be offered. The theologian Henri Nouwen calls this "healing":

> So healing is the receiving and full understanding of the story so that strangers can recognize in the eyes of their host their own unique way that leads them to the present and suggests the direction in which to go.[11]

As people have known for ages, stories help us to remain human, as they touch our spirit. The healing nature of telling and receiving stories, sharing our vulnerabilities and imperfections, is the foundation of the most common form of modern communal healing in the world—support groups like Alcoholics Anonymous.[12] In my experience as a participant in Al-Anon, I and the others simply shared stories, our own vulnerability connecting us to the vulnerability of others in compassionate and loving ways. I saw how people needed to tell their stories, to listen to others' stories, and to feel that they've been listened to. This simple process is the mystery of healing and becoming whole. These groups are similar to the ways in which community healing has occurred in diverse cultures throughout much of human history.[13]

Heartful communities are environments in which all can bring forth their abilities, creating a space where listeners can thrive, one that is patient and quiet and in which they can think deeply before they speak. We do not assume that an "open discussion" brings forth everyone's voice. So we provide ways to include the valuable ideas of those who appreciate silence or even feel silenced. We do this by putting ideas into writing before meeting, and by taking turns at talking.

In our development of heartful leadership capacities, we stress that while leaders must take action, they need to understand before they act to achieve the outcomes they desire. They have to listen to their peers, subordinates, customers, competitors, and all others whom they care about. In design thinking, there is a similar principle of empathizing through listening to customers, to understand what their true needs are.

Leaders have to ask their people how they can become even better leaders and then must listen, so that they may learn whether they're leading in the right or the wrong direction. If they are truly open, they may even learn what followers think of their leadership. Listening may be the most important leadership skill.[14]

Heartful communities value the effort to understand with sincerity, as a way of helping others feel better and change their attitudes, moods, and behaviors. Emotional understanding of others is directly linked to our awareness and understanding of ourselves. We can be good listeners if we open our hearts and minds to the messages of others, ask questions of them, focus on what they are saying, and treat them with respect. In doing so, we learn new ideas and build good relationships, with friends, family members, and coworkers.

If we can listen to another person, we begin to see the world from their viewpoint, reducing tension, preventing trouble, and solving problems. We know the benefit when we ourselves tell someone about a problem or situation that is bothering us or causing distress and when they listen and accept what we are saying without judgment. Being listened to may even be cathartic, cleansing, or healing and may enhance our well-being. The power of telling our stories is supported by research showing how a story activates parts of the brain that allow listeners to turn the story into their own ideas and experiences.[15]

The Zen monk Thich Nhat Hanh calls "deep listening" a sacred activity—a form of surrendering, receiving, letting in, in which you listen with one sole purpose: to let the other person empty his heart. When you listen with compassion, you give the person a chance to suffer less. This may not change the person, but you have established a foundation of empathy and communication. If you want to help him to correct his perception, you have to wait for another time when he is open to listening to you. Nhat Hanh believes that we get to this place of listening through practice:

> Listening is a very deep practice ... you have to empty yourself. You have to leave space in order to listen ... especially to people we think are our enemies—the ones we believe are making our situation worse.... When you have shown your capacity for listening and understanding, the other person will begin to listen to you and you have a chance to tell him or her of your pain, and it's your turn to be healed. This is the practice of peace.[16]

He warns us that the wrong perceptions that we have of self and others lead to fear, anger, and despair—the foundations of conflict, war, and violence. If we can start with a sincere desire to know others' suffering, they will open their heart and tell us what they are feeling, creating the possibility of correcting their perceptions as well as our own. Compassionate listening can be a way toward relieving the suffering of an individual—even changing the world for the better.

Yoshiko, my hospice client, was one of many teachers from whom I have learned that listening is a way to experience the beauty and wonder of being alive that is heartfulness. Being with other persons in a state of mindfulness—simply being present, maybe even silent—is good enough, and healing. Compassion arises if we can breathe, be unafraid, not escaping from the reality of the situation, and suffering together. We can express love in the desire to respond to another's needs, to the best of our ability.

EXERCISES

I. Passive Listening

A brief exercise in listening without verbally responding can be insightful in understanding our habitual patterns of communication.

1. Ask someone you know if they would like to do a listening exercise. One person is the talker and the other is the listener.
2. The talker talks about a current issue in their life (preferably not too upsetting) for 3 minutes. The listener simply listens, without talking.
3. Then reverse roles.
4. When finished, reflect on how each of you felt as talker and listener.

II. Active Listening

Listening is a skill that can be strengthened with practice.

1. Review the steps of active listening in this chapter.

2. When you are with someone and notice they want to talk, take the role of the listener.
3. Practice the steps of active listening in your dialogue. Avoid talking a lot, giving advice, or having an ordinary back-and-forth conversation.
4. Sometime after finishing, write about your reflections on the experience for 10 minutes.

6
ACCEPTANCE

This being human is a guest house. Every morning a new arrival. A joy, a depression, a meanness, some momentary awareness comes as an unexpected visitor. Welcome and attend them all! Even if they're a crowd of sorrows, who violently sweep your house empty of all its furniture, still, treat each guest honorably. He may be clearing you out for some new delight.[1]

—RUMI

Shizuko was 43 years old, in the mid-stages of ALS and losing voluntary control of her body. The first time I sat by her bedside and talked to her, I became aware of an intense feeling of fear inside myself. I wondered what it was like for her, living inside that crippled body. I struggled to be mindful, but kept imagining how beautiful she must have been and how tragic it was that her body was now being ravaged by such a debilitating disease.

Despite her deterioration, Shizuko always smiled when we were together. I was confused and doubted her sincerity at first. Why wasn't she crying? Why wasn't she raging against her cruel fate? Instead, she expressed gratitude and appreciation for the doctors, the nurses, her family, me, and the good life with which she was blessed.

Shizuko became my teacher. When she sensed that I was scared for her, she would look into my eyes and say softly, "You know, we are not just our bodies." As we sat there together, my hand resting in hers, we would occasionally fall into a peaceful silence.

With her kindness and compassion, she calmed my fears.

I knew that something profound was happening through my relationship with Shizuko. Was I being awakened by a deep sense of awareness of our connection as humans? Was I discovering that inside her body, as in all our bodies, a soul was ripe to be free? I felt the anxiety subside in me, bathed in her peaceful radiance. Shizuko helped free me of my fearful response to such severely disabling conditions as hers.

While I still cannot imagine what it is like to live in a body like Shizuko's day after day, she showed me the possibility of seeing beyond the visible physical realities. Awakening to a different worldview can make even such an extreme, seemingly tragic life rich in its moment-to-moment beauty. Seeing Shizuko gracefully embrace the profound physical changes in her life gave me an appreciation for the resilience of the human spirit.

Shizuko was accepting her fate. She couldn't change it, but she could choose how to live with that reality. We constantly struggle with wanting life to be a certain way rather than dealing with the way it really is. As our lives unfold, we resist entering fully into the stream of present moments as they are unfolding. Instead, we engage in a process of forcing, resisting, longing. What would our lives be like if we could only allow things to be as they are? As Victor Frankl said of those in the Nazi death camps, "When they were unable to change their situation, they were challenged to change themselves."[2]

Heartfulness involves balancing this tension between accepting things as they are and working to make them better. Life teaches us that there are so many things that can't be controlled through willpower. No matter how successful we are, there are still things beyond our power to determine. Our challenge is to accept reality, surrender to what's happening, and trust that everything will be all right, that no matter what happens we will be able to deal with it. Acceptance moves us to be kind to ourselves and others, to come alive through responsible action.

Shizuko was showing me gentleness, an attitude of letting be, patiently abiding with herself, her situation, her fate, her trials. She was taking herself and her world as they were—while teaching me that even when you are suffering, you can still believe that life is good, that simply being alive is good. She was showing unconditional presence, opening to whatever she was experiencing, no matter how challenging it was. I sensed that this allowed her life to unfold in the direction of greater freedom, truth, and wisdom.

If I had asked Shizuko why she went on, perhaps she would have answered like the physician and author Paul Kalanithi, who was dying of cancer at 37: "The secret is to know that the deck is stacked, that you will lose, that your hands or judgment will slip, and yet still struggle to win."[3] Shizuko accepted, more than most of us, that while we can't control what happens or reach perfection, we *can* believe in a purpose toward which we ceaselessly strive.

Acceptance in Japanese Culture

Shizuko was probably raised as I was, with a *shikata ga nai* mentality that permeated everything in life. Literally, the phrase means that nothing can be done and so it's no use asking or complaining. What one desires just isn't possible. Pouting is not an option. *Shikata ga nai* means that it does no good to wallow in self-pity or whining. The message is to get over it and move on to doing what you *can* do, appreciating what you have, rather than longing for what you don't have.

Kiyo Morimoto, the mentor I have mentioned previously, grew up on a potato farm in Idaho with parents who had immigrated from Wakayama, Japan. When the war broke out in the Pacific in 1941, at age 24 he enlisted in the U.S. Army and became part of the celebrated 442nd Regimental Combat Unit that fought in Europe. For Kiyo, this was both a source of pride and sadness, because the horrors of war inflicted deep wounds and scars on him.

While Kiyo and other young men responded by committing themselves to fight for their country, many of the older generation reacted by accepting the situation of being sent to incarceration camps by the U.S. government, implicitly saying, *"shikata ga nai."* As a youth, this response by his elder Japanese (Issei) had frustrated and angered him, feeling it was passive resignation, just giving up rather than fighting. But as he grew older he came to see it differently, as a way of coping with the things in life that cannot be changed. It is a way of accepting and even embracing one's vulnerability and helplessness. And it is from this acceptance that people are freed from the chains of their victimization and enabled to claim the agency to move on. *Shikata ga nai* is a way by which people feel new energy that can be directed into creative and productive activities, living with appreciation and gratitude rather than bitterness and regret. It is a way of acceptance that can lead to change. Accepting what can't be changed can, paradoxically, produce the courage to change what one can. Kiyo wrote:

> By recognizing and acknowledging where we are, we discover new possibilities and freedoms within the limits of the immediate context in which we find ourselves. The Issei, by owning and respecting their helplessness, directed their energy within the barrenness of the relocation centers, to grow and to nurture lovely flower and vegetable gardens; to write powerful poetry; and to create exquisite works of art. They knew that every day was a gift of life. For what is more precious than life? It is God's gift to us, to be lived with dignity and with love.[4]

Japanese-American men like Kiyo responded to the desperate situation of war by laying their lives on the line for their country and their community. Others responded by resisting and protesting injustice, refusing to fight for the United States. And most of the older generation went quietly to the "relocation" camps. Each way of responding was courageous, showing the power of the human spirit to cope and even thrive in the most difficult situations in our lives. *Shikata ga nai* means resilience, making the best of the situation. After the incarcerated were released, many discovered that all of their property was lost, so they put their energy into rebuilding their lives and guiding their children in becoming successful, responsible members of society.

Shikata ga nai is connected with the Buddhist concept of *dukkha,* meaning suffering, and the reality that life does not always go as we wish. When I first heard this as a child, I thought it was too pessimistic to state that life is suffering. It threatened the fragile optimism that I strove to nourish. But, growing up, I have faced the reality that there are things in life that we cannot avoid and that it is always good to identify the truth of the human condition.

This is not a popular way of thinking; people want to be happy, hopeful, and optimistic. People today want to believe that life is fun. We have an industry of self-help books and a field of positive psychology that teaches us how to be happy and successful. We can learn ways of thinking, doing, and being that enhance our well-being. But even this field is endorsing the Dalai Lama's call to embrace life in its wholeness rather than simply striving for happiness:

> Most people in modern Western society tend to go through life believing that the world is basically a nice place to live, life is mostly fair, and that they are good people who deserve to have good things happen to them. These beliefs can play an important role in leading a happier and healthier life. But the inevitable arising of suffering undermines these beliefs and can make it difficult to go on living happily and effectively.[5]

Life is full of inevitable suffering and necessary losses that often challenge our beliefs in fairness and goodness. We may feel despair when we encounter experiences in our everyday lives that are beyond our control. Like many others, throughout my life, I have found that raging against the helplessness of that which I can't control doesn't do any good. Peace and tranquility have come in accepting the challenges I face with heartfulness. Being mindful of my vulnerability, surrendering to the mystery, I compassionately move on with others, grateful for what I *do* have.

Perseverance in Japanese Culture

Another heartful way of coping that Japanese people use is *ganbaru.* Following the earthquake, tsunami, and nuclear plant disaster in northern Japan in 2011, many well-intentioned people rushed in to help with a simple message: *"ganbatte!"* The concept of *ganbaru* is deeply rooted in Japanese culture as an approach to life. It's often used in daily language to encourage others to "do your best," to "fight on!" and to "never give up!" whether at work, playing in a sporting event, or studying for an exam. While one does not always have to win, one must never give up, persevering with tenacity until the end.

While others may encourage you with a cheer of *"ganbatte kudasai!,"* the real spirit of *ganbaru* comes from within. Psychologists call this kind of motivation "intrinsic motivation," distinguishing it from "extrinsic motivation" that comes from outside ourselves. Intrinsic motivation means that for the benefit of oneself—and for the benefit of others, as well—one must bear down and do one's best. This mentality teaches that in a crisis, one should not complain, act selfishly, or cry over what might have been; while these feelings may be natural, they are not productive for oneself or for others. *Ganbaru* is heartful, as it pushes us to engage in responsible action.

The saying *"Nana-Korobi, Ya-Oki"* (Fall seven times, get up eight) is a Japanese proverb that reflects the ideal of resilience. No matter how many times you get knocked down, you get up again. You can see this ethic reinforced in all facets of Japanese culture, including education, business, sports, and martial arts. It is especially important to remember the sentiment expressed in this proverb when times are dark. There are no quick fixes in life, and anything of real worth will necessarily take struggle and perseverance. What's important is to simply do your best and persist.

"Nana-Korobi, Ya-Oki" stresses that while successful people don't always win and suffer setbacks like everyone else, they don't give up. They keep trying, seeing challenges as opportunities, not as problems. This ability to recover and grow stronger is intrinsic to a culture that not only values personal responsibility and hard work but also embraces humility and a sense of belonging and contributing to a community.

When I visited the tsunami disaster area in 2011, I met a man who embodied the philosophy of heartfulness. His wife and son had perished, and, wanting to understand how people live after suffering such losses, I asked him how he faces each day. He smiled and said that first he remembers his wife and son, feeling both the loss and the continued connection. He reflects on the incredible mystery of living and tells himself: "I am alive and my life is precious, so I don't want to waste it; I will use all my energies to be good to myself, and to give to others. And then I get moving and do what I can."

What he *can* do is simply to listen to others with compassion and act responsibly. He told me that the message of *ganbatte* is powerful and, while there is a time when it is appropriate, his fellow survivors were not always receptive to this message. So he allowed them to express their true feelings and did his best to offer them his presence. For many, *shikata ga nai* is a natural response to tragedy that allows them to embrace their helplessness. For others, *ganbatte* may be the message they need to hear when the time is right.

The calm, patient, orderly behavior following the disasters in Japan that won praise from all over the world reflects a *shikata ga nai* view of nature. The feeling of awe toward nature and embracing a way of respectful coexistence may come from the repeated earthquakes and other natural disasters the Japanese have experienced from earliest times. By witnessing the death and suffering of innocent people, the Japanese have come to understand their helplessness in the face of nature's upheavals.

One way of coping has been through writing. After the Great Hanshin-Awaji Earthquake of 1995, in their desperate circumstances, the people of the disaster area composed hundreds of haiku. So, too, in the aftermath of the 2011 disaster, many people sought refuge in poetry. The story of tsunami survivor Isao Sato, a resident of Iwate Prefecture that was devastated by the March 2011 tsunami, is one example.[6]

He comments: "From out of the blue, a huge tsunami came and washed away my home and all the material possessions I had worked for my whole life. But when I finally came to myself, I looked around and realized that I still had my family, and that this year, once again, the world was filled with the sweet, fresh breeze of early summer." He composed this haiku:

Bereft of belongings
Yet blessed by the touch of the
Early summer breeze.

In this haiku we see a beautiful expression of how loss can give birth to gratitude for what remains. As if awakening from a bad dream, the poet feels the wonder of the breeze, bringing an awareness that he has survived the tragedy and is alive. Life goes on. Focusing on the beauty of the breeze is an act of courage that creates a new consciousness and will to live, overwhelming the feelings of hopelessness and helplessness. This enduring faith in nature, despite the tragedies it brings, became a source of inspiration not only for the victims but also for people everywhere in Japan who, like all humans, must exist in an uncertain world.

The value of trusting in nature and accepting things as they are, not the way we want them to be, is deeply rooted in Japanese cultural traditions based on philosophies of acceptance. Zen and indigenous therapies, such as Morita and Naikan, teach that acceptance—surrendering to that which is beyond our control—paradoxically liberates the spirit to move on. Resignation has a place in human development, and change is not inevitably a positive and good outcome.

The power of this way of coping is reinforced by scientific studies that show how well-being is enhanced when we focus on the positive rather than the negative. For example, one recent study showed that people who expressed gratitude daily felt more positive affect, had stronger social relationships, and coped better with stress and adversity.[7]

Because of my family background, I have often viewed the concept of acceptance with an East-West perspective, realizing that it is overly general and simplistic. My upbringing in America valued action and change, while my Japanese cultural influence encouraged acceptance. Balancing the two is an ongoing struggle for me, as it is for everyone. We each balance our tendencies to proactively assert ourselves or to go with the flow, accepting what life is bringing us. We know that both ways have their time and place. The art of living is knowing which way is called for in any particular moment. When I go with the flow,

Americans generally see this as passive, while Japanese paradoxically acknowledge it as active. It is a way of moving through life, striving to do our best from day to day, trusting that everything will be all right—respecting the complexity, ambiguity, and uncertainty in our existence. Recognizing when going with the flow is an excuse requires summoning the courage to act. Heartfulness is a way of reaching this understanding by being mindfully aware of what we are truly feeling and being compassionate and responsible to ourselves and others.

"Balance" has different meanings. In the United States, it means changing or transcending inconsistencies to avoid dissonance. In Japan, balance is often described as asymmetrical, defined by tolerating inconsistency and dissonance rather than resolving differences. In this view, many problems resolve themselves without our having to take a stand, because in fact we human beings are never in complete control. There are times when trusting in powers beyond ourselves, we might arrive at a better resolution than we would by rushing to judgment and action.

One way of understanding balance and mixed-ness is through the Taoist philosophy of yin and yang. These contrasting but complementary forces of female and male principles are expressed as a balance that recognizes the necessary presence of both light and dark to provide meaning. That balance is a harmonious tension between these principles. Humans are a part of a dynamic order and relational design in which all elements serve a necessary function. Applied to our daily lives, having a sense of balance means touching the deepest existential questions in our lives as well as dealing with mundane tasks while developing a full capacity for joy and sadness, a view of well-being supported by scientific research.[8]

The Serenity Prayer

Acceptance is often equated with Buddhism, yet there is a Christian message of acceptance in the Serenity Prayer of theologian Reinhold Niebuhr.

*God grant me the serenity to accept the things I cannot change,
The courage to change the things I can,
And the wisdom to know the difference.*

The prayer teaches us to find comfort in the reality that there are things in life that simply must be accepted because they cannot be changed. To put one's energy into changing the unchangeable is deadening to the human spirit. This is not a prayer of passive resignation or defeat. Rather, it calls for courage to change what *can* be changed—doing what one can in the situation one is in. Action is called for if something can be done.

So, when do we know that we are no longer able to change a situation? Certain things in life, such as natural disasters, injuries, illnesses, and all things that have already occurred, are without question unchangeable. Yet there can be great questioning of what actually *can* be changed. The ancient Greek philosopher Epictetus wrote:

Make the best use of what is in your power, and take the rest as it happens. Some things are up to us and some things are not up to us. Our opinions are up to us, and our impulses, desires, aversions—in short, whatever is our own doing. Our bodies are not up to us, nor are our possessions, our reputations, or our public offices, or, that is, whatever is not our own doing.[9]

As with the criticism of *shikata ga nai* as too passive, the emphasis in the Serenity Prayer on acceptance strikes some people as resignation in the face of adversity. Another version, which is more action-oriented, requests "courage to change" before asking for serenity: *"Father, give us courage to change what must be altered, serenity to accept what cannot be helped, and the insight to know the one from the other."*

The third part of the prayer—finding the wisdom to know the difference—is difficult. How do we know the difference? A later and longer version of the prayer includes the following, which provides useful guidelines:

*Living one day at a time,
Enjoying one moment at a time,
Accepting hardship as a pathway
to peace.*

This is a message of heartfulness, living mindfully, appreciating the world as it is, rather than desiring it to be different. This is not an easy thing, especially for young people, or for privileged people who are used to having things their way, owning the resources to fulfill many of their desires. For many of us, our idealism and painful awareness of how things are not the way they should be can cause us to disengage or despair. When we do not get everything we want in life, learning to face our own personal weaknesses and brokenness becomes a great challenge; we may feel overwhelmed and hopeless about changing our circumstances, or ourselves.

It is in these moments that the principles of heartfulness that we have reflected on so far—beginner's mind, vulnerability, authenticity, connectedness, listening—all come into play. We learn to live moment-by-moment, being imperfectly human, being who we truly are. Living is *good* when we connect with others by seeing and hearing them.

Feeling the joy of living is possible, even though we don't have everything figured out or all our desires met. We can be reasonably happy, appreciating the moment and its wonder, reminding ourselves of our limitations, with a humble awareness that we are not the center of the universe. Heartfulness is learning how to live in a world where things are not ideal or perfect.

I have always struggled to see acceptance as an active way of dealing with the mundane aspects of life—daily tasks, studying, washing, cooking, working. Dwelling in my typical world of idealism paralyzes my ability to do meaningful work or pursue real relationships. I am forced to surrender illusions of what the world should be, and tell myself that what I have is okay and that what I have to offer—like writing this book or teaching a class—is enough. Acceptance frees me to pursue real-life expectations and goals daily, by bringing me closer to a feeling of being connected with the world around me, engaging actively with the pain and even the boredom that accompany reality.

There is often pushback against the concept of acceptance by some youths who see it as resignation. At political events I often see signs with a message attributed to the feminist Angela Davis: *"I am no longer accepting the things I cannot change; I am changing the things I cannot accept."* Acceptance requires surrender, another word (like "vulnerability") that we often think of negatively. But how do we surrender? Religious people have an answer—they trust in God. Nonreligious people, by contrast, are called to think of their purpose for being created and alive, to see their life as learning to live gracefully amid complete uncertainty.

A heartful approach is expressed by Ram Dass and Mirabai Bush:

> Compassion in action is paradoxical and mysterious. It is absolute yet continually changing. It accepts that everything is happening exactly as it should, and

it works with a full-hearted commitment to change. It sets goals but knows that the process is all there. It is joyful in the midst of suffering and hopeful in the face of overwhelming odds. It is simple in a world of complexity and confusion. It is done for others but nurtures the self. It shields in order to be strong. It intends to eliminate suffering, knowing that suffering is endless. It is action arising from emptiness.[10]

The wisdom sought in the Serenity Prayer is discovered somewhere in the space between the extremes of the paradox of being human—nothing, and everything. There we confront our helplessness and woundedness and can see more clearly what is to be accepted and what is to be changed. But understanding this difference is complicated by our personal histories of power, privilege, and victimization. A history of being victimized may give us a consciousness that leads to assumptions that things cannot be changed, trapping us by self-limiting beliefs.

Beyond our personal concerns, the problems that the world presents us may seem insurmountable because simply struggling for our own survival consumes so much of our time and energy. We view ourselves as victims rather than embracing the power within us to change our reality. We are called to move out of this way of thinking of ourselves as victims, by recognizing the power to act that is in our own hands.

The need to overcome our crippling sense of victimization was also voiced by Martin Luther King, Jr.:

> We need to see ourselves not mainly as victims but as new men and women who, recognizing the sacredness in ourselves and in others, can view love and compassion not as some "sentimental weakness" but as the key that somehow unlocks the door which leads to ultimate reality.[11]

Morita Therapy

My search for understanding acceptance has brought me to the work of Shoma Morita, a contemporary of

Freud and Jung, yet a psychiatrist with radically different ideas influenced by Zen training.[12] Morita believed that the acceptance of one's true nature was an essential step in healing. Rather than trying to change oneself, one should let nature takes its course. Morita asserted that trying to control or use reason to eliminate disturbing and recurring thoughts only intensifies them, making us even more sensitive to them. He taught that by acknowledging that there are facts of life and nature that cannot be changed with willpower, we can then accept that fact and be at peace. He urged his patients to tolerate pain and not be stopped by obsessive, disturbing thoughts or by trying to actively get rid of their symptoms; the process of recovery, he believed, is not to will our symptoms away but to allow recovery to happen spontaneously.

Morita taught that the path to good living is by:
    Knowing what one is doing,
    Knowing what the situation is requiring,
    Knowing the relationship between the two.

In this way of healing, character is developed by cultivating mindfulness, knowing what is controllable and what is not controllable, and seeing what is real without attachment to expectations. Morita's patients were guided in directing their attention receptively to what reality brings in each moment, focusing on the present, and avoiding intellectualizing. As in *shikata ga nai,* acceptance of what *is* allows for active responding to what needs doing. Similar to the message in the Serenity Prayer, distinguishing between what can and can't be changed is crucial.

The power of Morita therapy comes from facing the difficulty of simply accepting things as they are, when we are conditioned to constantly try to exert our will to control life's external conditions. Trying to control may sometimes be good, because in certain cases things *can* be controlled. But this willful way leads us astray when we confront things that can't be controlled, such as when we try to control other people—what they think of us, what they feel, or what they do. In these cases, we can learn that life can't always be the way we want it and to simply accept what *is.* We come to see that people can't be who we want them to be, so we accept them for who they are.

Morita's philosophy expresses heartfulness. This is a gentle way of being—not acting too willfully; not forcing ourselves, others, or situations; taking ourselves and our world as is; allowing others to be who they are, not forcing them to change. We accept the limited but precious beings we are, and we extend the same gentleness to others. We try not to harm ourselves by self-condemnation, which may injure our finer sensitivities or silence our better self.

The concept of *arugamama* expresses this heartful way of living with the dynamic tension created by acceptance and the desire for change. It is a state of unconditional acceptance of yourself and your life as they are at this moment, with the simultaneous intention to act in positive ways to create change. There is a gentleness to accepting yourself as "good enough," rather than wallowing in self-criticism and the feeling of never being good enough.

This approach of self-compassion accepts the fluctuations of our thoughts and feelings, and grounds our behavior both in reality and in the purpose of the moment. Instead of focusing on alleviating discomfort or attaining an ideal feeling state, Morita's approach is heartful in stressing that we should take constructive action that helps us to live a full, meaningful existence. It is not a passive, resigned state of acceptance, but rather one that is energized and forward-looking.

Acceptance and change are intricately linked—for acceptance of what cannot be changed automatically leads to the courage to change what *can* be changed. Constructive action is not stopped while we cope with symptoms or feelings. This is an expression of true heartfulness—character is developed and healing occurs by what we do, putting compassion into action. We call on bravery and empower ourselves through decisions grounded in purpose and responsibility, rather than being influenced by the fluid flow of feelings.

In much of my training in Western psychological therapies, my colleagues and I learned to see the deficits in clients and to seek to improve them, to change them for the better. We were taught to strive to reduce symptoms, and to "repair" clients, as if they were objects to be fixed if only we could find the right parts. Change, by moving toward a solution and reconciling ambiguity, was our counseling goal.

Yet my clinical experience told me that striving for change was not always the right way, or the only way. Sometimes change occurred by not striving for it. Happiness research tells us that we may be happier by not striving for it.[13]

Over time I learned that trust was developed when I let the other person be. I learned this when I practiced the humanistic, person-centered therapy of Carl Rogers, who noticed the strange paradox that when he could accept himself just as he was, then he could change. I similarly observed clients change when they learned they can be respected for who they are, *as* they are. Those were the times that gave them hope that they could find new possibilities in life. Rogers' method was to accept the other person without judgment, rather than trying to treat, cure, or change them, asking only how he as therapist could provide a relationship that the person may use for his own personal growth.[14]

A heartful approach to psychotherapy is respecting people for who they are rather than seeing them as deficient until they become who I want them to be. We can let people be in the space between aggressive change and passive acceptance, honoring their vulnerability and the limitations their culture places on them. Seeking a balance of values of individual satisfaction with respect for family and society, we also balance personal responsibility for present actions with awareness of the blame that can be attributed to others and society itself for our problems.

The most common form of expressing heartfulness in which acceptance is practiced therapeutically every day is in support groups. In these informal gatherings, people who are suffering from the same or similar affliction come together to share stories. There is no professional therapist, only a facilitator. These groups promote a message of acceptance every day in hundreds of countries around the world. They are a source of empowerment for many people through accepting one's vulnerability.[15]

Letting Go

Meeting people like Shizuko, the ALS sufferer I was attending, has helped me to embrace the reality that accepting whatever comes our way is a key to the art of living. And one thing that most certainly comes our way is loss. My own aging teaches me that the challenge of coping with loss never goes away and reappears every day. So one day, when a high school student asked me, "What is the hardest thing in your life?" I answered without hesitating, "Letting go."

We grow to love certain things and people. Still, things change. We suffer losses—some necessary, some not. Letting go of what we desire is a hard lesson to learn, whether it's something from the past or something imagined in the future. We also have to learn to let go of what we are not meant to have. But how do you let go of what you love the most? You love your children and you love parenting them, but they have to grow up and someday will no longer need you and can function autonomously. This is the way of nature. You have to let go. Your body ages; you let go of youth. Our challenge is to find how to gracefully let go.

Some people draw comfort from these words in the Bible, popularized in a song: *"To every thing there is a season, and a time to every purpose under the heaven."*[16] Letting go is ceasing to cling to anything—whether it be a person, a pet, an idea, a thing, an event, a particular time, a view, or a desire. It is a conscious decision to fully enter into the stream of present moments as they are unfolding. Letting go means to give up forcing, resisting, or struggling. Instead, we may get something more powerful and wholesome by allowing things to be as they are without our becoming caught up in our attraction to or rejection of them.

I was moved at one of my son's high school graduation ceremony when some students sang an inspired version of the Rolling Stones' song:

> You can't always get what you want (repeating):
> You can't always get what you want...
> but if you try sometimes, you just might find
> you get what you need.[17]

Their enthusiasm for the lyrics might have been due to their increasing awareness that there are so many things in life that they can't control through willpower alone. No matter how successful they become, there will still be things in their lives whose outcome is beyond their power to determine. The youths were shouting out that they knew they can't always get what they want, or have everything go their way, but they *can* still try to get what they need.

Heartful parenting and teaching encourage and empower youth to learn that the times when we feel most profoundly changed and "grown-up" are the times when we adjust to not getting what we want. At those moments, there is a life lesson to be learned if we can accept reality, surrender to what's happening, and trust that everything will be all right—that, no matter what happens, we will be able to deal with it. We can move on in life with patience, receptiveness, and openness to the reality that change not only occurs through action but also springs from acceptance. We can tell ourselves and others that we are good just as we are—and that we can become better.

EXERCISES

I. *Flow or Row?*

Reflect on the following questions and write down your thoughts in a notebook:
1. What is something I need to accept?
2. What is something I need courage to change?
3. What is something that worked out well because I decided to "go with the flow," or let go of my desire to actively change the situation?
4. What is something that worked out well because I decided to "row," or act assertively?

II. *Serenity and Courage*

Reflect on the words of the Serenity Prayer:
>*Grant me the serenity to accept the things I cannot change,*
>*The courage to change the things I can,*

And the wisdom to know the difference.

1. Think of a time when something happened in your life that was beyond your control and you felt helpless or vulnerable. How did you accept the situation? Write down your thoughts for 10 minutes.
2. Think of a time when something happened and you felt control over the situation. How did you get the courage to take action? Write down your thoughts for 10 minutes.
3. Reflect on how you know the difference between what can be changed and what can't. Write down your thoughts for 5 minutes.

7

GRATITUDE

We learned about gratitude and humility—that so many people had a hand in our success, from the teachers who inspired us to the janitors who kept our school clean ... and we were taught to value everyone's contribution and treat everyone with respect.[1]
—MICHELLE OBAMA

Once a great talker, my Grandmother Mitsu spoke less and less as she neared the end of her 111 years on Earth. I knew that I would see her again, but as we were leaving her for what they thought would be their last visit, my wife and sister became emotional and apologized for not visiting more often. But Grandmother just waved her hand as if to say, "no worries, it's okay," putting her hands prayerfully together in *gassho,* saying *arigatou,* an expression of thanks, and bowing her head.

When she fell into a coma and was "nearing the mountaintop," I rushed back to Japan to see her. When I called her name, she opened her eyes to see me and soon after refused food and water, and within hours there was silence. "She waited for you," the priest told me.

We took her body to the mountain village where she was born and where our family had donated land for the temple. As her closest relative, I was handling the proceedings. My mourning was consumed by attending to the details of the necessary rituals. As I paused to warm myself by the stove in the chilly temple, I noticed a poster on the wall showing a young woman pausing before eating to say grace, with the words *arigatou kara hajimeyoo* (let's begin with giving thanks). I felt that we were in the right place to honor my grandmother's spirit.

She had helped me to see life through the lens of gratitude, though throughout my whole life I have fallen short in this regard. I was an adolescent who at times did not appreciate being alive. I often thought of what could be and compared reality with an imagined world that I never attained and knew was unattainable. I struggled to live in the moment and took so much for granted. Yet I yearned to quiet my restless dissatisfaction, sensing that the transition to adulthood involves finding gratitude. My grandmother taught me how much better life was when I could be grateful. Living with her in my twenties, I began to feel a sense of contentment with my day-to-day existence and had a glimpse into the truth of finding meaning in the mundane, moments in which we feel the joy of being alive.

The image of heartfulness comes to me now when I see how mindfulness is intimately linked with gratitude. Being awake and aware of the "gift" of each moment fills us with appreciation, cultivating a grateful heart. If we are truly awake, then the mystery and wonder of each moment is apparent. Awareness of how much we are receiving can seem like a miracle, as expressed in the *kanji* for *arigatou* that portray the meaning of the expression of deep wonder and awe at what one has received.

In her healthy years, my grandmother's day began with offerings of fresh water and rice for our ancestors at the family altar (drinkers got a little sake). Then she prepared our breakfast and, before we ate, we gave thanks for the food we were receiving. She taught me to give thanks for all the small kindnesses bestowed on us every day. When I complained, she patiently taught me to appreciate what I had rather than regretting what I didn't have.

Grandmother's way of living expressed a sense of gratitude and trust toward the gods, our ancestors, and the people around us. Simple expressions of gratitude were part of daily life, as they are for many others today in Japan: the custom of saying *itadakimasu,* "I gratefully receive," before eating; the word *mottainai,* which conveys an aversion to waste; *okagesama de,* expressing gratitude to others for our good fortune. Some people in Japan may be unaware of the deeper meaning of these ritual sayings, so it is good to be reminded that these expressions arise from a deep-seated, subconscious understanding that we share the world with other living beings.

Many people these days seem to suffer from the belief that we are all individuals with boundaries, separate from others. Our Western cultures tell us that our purpose is to work to improve ourselves and to produce something worthwhile. We may come to think we owe nothing to anyone. But if we are heartful we know that this is an illusion. We are in fact deeply interconnected—more like cells with a permeable membrane, living by exchange and depending on other cells' lives. The exchange is continuous and determines both what we are and how we live. Gratitude, then, is a realistic view of what we are in relation to others.

In heartfulness, our interconnectedness means that we are responsible for each other. My grandmother emphasized that gratefulness naturally includes responsibility. I often wanted to know what I would *get* out of expressing gratitude, but she said it must be done with no expectation of reciprocity. She constantly reminded me of my responsibility as one who was receiving so much, to always give back, not necessarily to the same people from whom I received but sometimes to the next generation and society at large.

I also found this sentiment in Albert Einstein's writing:

> Without some deeper reflection one knows from daily life that one exists for other people—first of all for those upon whose smiles and well-being our own happiness is

wholly dependent, and then for the many, unknown to us, to whose destinies we are bound by the ties of sympathy. A hundred times every day I remind myself that my inner and outer life are based on the labors of other men, living and dead, and that I must exert myself in order to give in the same measure as I have received and am still receiving.[2]

My grandmother, and Einstein too, described a heartful way of being in which they were aware of and attentive as to how much there was to be grateful for in their daily lives. When my grandmother honored her ancestors or when Einstein reminded himself every day how much his life depended on others, they were being heartful.

The *kanji* for *kansha* 感謝 (gratitude) contains a heart, showing the feeling of thanks and also apology, thus the realization that someone or something has done something for you. This epitomizes the focus on interconnectedness, which is not as clearly included in the Latin root of the word "gratitude," *gratia,* which means grace, graciousness, gratefulness, as well as kindness, generosity, gifts, and the beauty of giving and receiving. But there may be a universal sense that gratitude arises from both receiving help from others and focusing habitually on the positive aspects of life. If we take to heart this way of being, we find the sources of gratitude are infinite, and include such mundane events as simply waking up in the morning, or appreciating one's abilities, or seizing a chance to do meaningful work. The object of gratitude may be humans, nonhuman animals, nature, God, or the universe, or all of these—with gratitude being part of a wider life orientation toward noticing and appreciating the positive things in the world.

I have discovered that across cultures and time, expressions of gratitude have been treated as basic and desirable aspects of human personality and social life. In many traditions, including Jewish, Christian, Muslim, Buddhist, and Hindu, gratitude is a virtue; their adherents have a common belief in the goodness of both feeling and expressing gratitude in response to received benefits. Many religious and spiritual groups encourage members to develop a worldview of one's life as a "gift," or of one's very self as being "blessed." The power of gratitude is expressed in a practical way in support groups and organizations, such as Alcoholics Anonymous, that are based on a belief that the regular practice of grateful thinking strengthens a sense of meaning for one's life.

I find that a heartful way of living requires daily rituals to remind us of the beauty of gratitude. A student from Dharamsala, India, the home to the Tibetan government-in-exile, gave me this prayer from His Holiness the Dalai Lama, which I recite first thing in the morning:

A Precious Human Life
Every day, think as you wake up

*"Today I am fortunate
To have woken up.
I am alive,
I have a precious human life.
I am not going to waste it.
I am going to use
All my energies to develop myself,*

*To expand my heart out to others,
To achieve enlightenment for
The benefit of all beings.
I am going to have
Kind thoughts toward others.
I am not going to get angry,
Or think badly about others.
I am going to benefit others
As much as I can."*[3]

Gratitude in Self-Reflection

Gratitude may come easily to us when we get what we want, but when difficulties come our way we are tested to maintain this positive attitude. This challenge is especially strong when we are confronted with illness. In my search for understanding how humans heal from illnesses of various kinds, I found *Naikan,* a therapeutic method based in gratitude.[4] Developed by Ishin Yoshimoto in Japan, Naikan draws on Eastern spiritual and psychological traditions. Naikan, meaning "to look inside," is a method of introspection, reflecting on one's life, one's relationships with others, and the impact we are having on the world around us.

Naikan asks three questions that provide a foundation for reflecting on relationships with others, such as parents, friends, and children. As we reflect on our relationships, one by one, we begin to gain a realistic view of our conduct and of the exchange that has occurred in the relationship:

"What have I received from the other person?"

"What have I given to the other person?"

"What troubles and difficulties have I caused others?"

Naikan fascinated me, because it offered such a contrasting view of healing from the psychotherapy I was learning in the United States. Rather than concentrate on ways in which we had been hurt by others, in Naikan there is no step of acknowledging the harm another person has done. Instead the focus is on how we have been helped by others, using our relationships with others as a mirror in which we can see ourselves. We reflect on what we have received from others, what we have given, and what troubles we have caused. When we think of everyone to whom we can feel grateful, we realize that all we possess has come to us from others or has been evoked by their presence.

Of course, the people to whom we may feel the most grateful are often those toward whom we also feel resentment, especially our parents. Our challenge is to concentrate on good aspects of their treatment of us, however small. We reflect further on what we have neglected in thoughtlessness or without consideration of the other person's existence.

Our human capacity for self-reflection is the root of our suffering, but it also holds a key to our freedom. A sincere examination of ourselves is a difficult task, requiring attention to our mistakes, failures, and weaknesses, and acknowledging our transgressions as well as actions that have caused difficulty to others.

Naikan does not permit blame or complaint about how we have been treated by others, as it is based in a belief that it is more productive to focus on ourselves. Well-being is related to our ability to maintain a worldview in which we realize how much we receive every day, every moment, that keeps us alive. As a psychotherapist, I notice how healthy people are not blaming others but instead are grateful. When a client feels gratitude, she is healing—neither overestimating nor underestimating herself, but being capable of seeing value in her situation and appreciating what is good in her life.

The discovery of Naikan gave me a new understanding of the power of gratefulness, of cultivating a grateful heart. Through its philosophy we may develop a natural and profound sense of gratitude for blessings bestowed on us by others, as well as a healthy desire to find meaning in our life and the inspiration to contribute to others' happiness and welfare. This is the way of heartfulness, focusing our energy on what we have received and also on what we can give in return. It directs energy first inward and then outward to others and to a greater good.

While Naikan is an intense form of therapy, we can practice its principles in daily life. I like to reflect on the same questions used in the therapy: "What have I received from the other person?" If this question proves to be too difficult, I try another: "What have I given to the other person?" Or I may ask, "What troubles and difficulties have I caused others?" This simple exercise, which can be practiced at any time and any place, provides great benefits of cultivating heartfulness.

This focus in Naikan on what others have done for you and how you have caused difficulties for others reveals a strikingly different way of viewing forgiveness than what is taught in mainstream psychology. But both stress that some things call for forgiveness, or making peace with the past and closing that part of our life. We do not need to condone or forget, and we are still careful that it does not happen again. We stop constantly investing parts of ourselves in the event and reliving things that are long past, and we cease feeding anger about the wrong. Forgiveness means living in the present moment, opening relations with others, and moving the energy from blame, hate, prejudice, and revenge into new, fruitful ways of living.

Of course, there is nothing more difficult to do, even if we know that research shows that those who forgive more easily enjoy better physical health and suffer less from anxiety and depression. Still, most people find it hard to move on from either a major injustice or minor slights, wallowing in victimization, attaching their identity to the wrong received. Change becomes impossible if our indignation supports our whole personality; we fear that we will lose our identity if we forgive.

To forgive, we need to recognize the wrong we have felt, the sometimes terrible suffering we may have yet to confront. Forgiveness means being less concerned with judgment and more with understanding. This demands humility and flexibility, leading to radical transformation of our personality. Before forgiving the injustice, we have to acknowledge and feel it fully. This is the paradox of forgiveness.[5]

Naikan offers an alternative heartful path of compassion, redirecting the energy devoted to trying to forgive others back to our own conduct and treatment of them. Focusing on the "sins" of others, condemning them for what they have done to us, nourishes resentment and anger in us.[6] Healing comes from accepting the reality of the things we ourselves have done to hurt others. Ultimately, we may find that we are in no position to grant forgiveness, and that we have received forgiveness without even asking for it.

This heartful approach pushes us to be moved to empathize with the person who has offended. If we manage to place ourselves in their situation, then understand their intentions and suffering as well as our own, we find it easier to forgive. We can understand why they did what they did. Perhaps the discovery that the cerebral activities of forgiveness and empathy take place in the same area of the brain should not surprise us. Yet we also know that forgiveness is truly a matter of the heart.

Gratitude in Illness

One way that I renew my sense of gratitude is by being with those who have come to a deep understanding through facing severe illness. Ana Stenzel, one of the twins mentioned earlier, regularly gave guest lectures for my classes before she passed away in September 2013. The previous autumn, Ana came to speak to my students, many of whom were planning to be health care providers. They listened attentively, deeply touched by her wisdom that was far beyond her years. That week, they wrote in their journals how much Ana had taught them about living with acceptance and appreciation for what we have been given. In class they talked about how the experience of Ana's sharing her story had given them the courage to live more fully with gratitude for the small things, accepting their own and others' frailties and vulnerabilities.

In July, two months before she died, Ana wrote this message of gratitude:

> By living alongside death for so long, I have truly lived. By being

aware of limited time, I have not wasted any time, my life has been better for it. Too bad it has taken illness to realize this. But what does every human being strive for? To me, everyone wishes to feel love and connection, to be part of something great, to make an impact, to be inspired, to leave the world with a sense of peace and satisfaction. Fortunately, thanks to great motivation and a backdrop for opportunity, all those things have landed in my lap. Our film and book have made an impact, exceptional people encircle me, and I have felt the love of God, of a spouse, of my young nieces, and even my new basset mix puppy, Timon. I have seen more stunning scenery through my travels than I ever dreamed of, and I felt the highest of highs and lowest of lows in human emotions. There are no regrets....[7]

Ana's mother, Hatsuko, gives us a parental perspective on gratitude when expectations are short for a child born with a terminal illness. On Ana's passing at age 41, Hatsuko's sadness was matched with joy from deep gratitude for the time that Ana had to accomplish so much. Ana had learned to appreciate the preciousness of each day, as had her mother. For Hatsuko, getting another month with her child, or another five years or even one year, was everything.

Ana writes how it took illness to teach her not to waste time and to be mindful of moments and grateful for opportunities. My colleague Barnett Pearce, who was dying of cancer, called his illness "a wake-up call" and jokingly wrote a memo to himself: "Don't make the universe shout so loud to get your attention next time!"[8]

I also learned about gratitude from two friends, a couple who went through end stages of cancer together. Soh was 71 years old when he died, just months after his wife, Chio, passed away at 65 in the same hospice in St. Luke's Hospital in Tokyo. Soh learned about gratitude caring for Chio through the final stages of her life after she had been diagnosed with lung cancer. He became her caretaker, dedicating his life to helping her battle her illness. But his task became infinitely more trying when he was diagnosed with stomach cancer the following year. Although he had expected to outlive her, suddenly he was concerned about whether he would be able to care for her until the end. Soh became both caretaker and fellow traveler, following along as Chio moved through stages of cancer, facing each challenge before he did. She became his teacher of living and dying, and especially of gratitude. They each kept a journal and, after her death, Soh put them together into a book.

This story of heartfulness shows how Chio's mindful living gave her such gratitude for everything. Chio writes that she sees even her cancer with gratitude, as an experience that enables her to connect with others' suffering. "Because we are having this strange experience I can empathize with the feeling of those who suffer, I can be one with them," she writes. When Chio comforts Soh by calling him her "comrade-in-arms," he realizes that his illness has bridged the gap that divides those with cancer from others, which gives him a peaceful feeling of oneness. They joined in compassion, as they suffered, truly together.

Chio tells Soh that she accepts all of life as her destiny and God's will. She is at peace. But Soh can't understand.

"How can you be so bright and cheerful when you have such a serious illness?" he asks.

She smiles and replies, "Because I am grateful for the kindness of those around me."

She gives thanks to those who care for her, thanks for beauty, thanks for truth. Chio, an artist, notices and acknowledges the small things in life as blessings—a simple meal of rice and miso soup, the nurses who serve her, those who deliver her food, visits from her sons and their wives, her natural medicine, her hospital medicine, morning exercise, reading a paper leisurely, and living at home like a "heroine with her partner."

Shortly before her death, Chio writes in her journal: "I may not be long in this world; it may be the terminal stage for me but every morning I am thankful for the gift of life, being able to take a deep breath of a flower's fragrance. Last night Soh told me that tomorrow is our wedding anniversary and he would buy me flowers. In bed, I wondered why I had received such a wonderful husband.... Thank you."

Soh accompanied Chio through the final stage of dying, interpreting her slight nod to his question, "Are you ready?" as a request for a life-terminating injection that delivered her from her agony. It was spring, and by autumn of that year Soh entered the same hospice.

Referring to his 44 years together with his wife, Chio, Soh wrote these words: "All that remains is gratitude."[9]

Soh lived heartfully till the end by making his last job the creation of a book that integrated the journals both he and Chio had kept in their final days. He saw this as fulfilling his responsibility to their love. He gave it as a gift to his friends, and it was eventually made into a book for the public, then a television program, and finally even an opera.

My friends' beautiful expressions of gratitude in the midst of suffering and dying have reinforced my grandmother's teachings of the samurai way of *Bushido*. I use these lessons through a daily ritual of reflecting on death, imagining my own death. This practice heightens awareness of the gift of life itself; each day then becomes a new thing—and the possibility of authentic living emerges.

Teaching and Parenting

Gratefulness permeated my upbringing. Going out with my dad was always an impressionable experience in my childhood. Wherever we went, he insisted on engaging with whoever was there—it didn't matter how "low" the person was on the social hierarchy, Dad treated everyone the same, as somebody worthy. He respected all people, in the sense of seeing them and modeling grateful behavior. I observed him as he greeted people working in the street, picking up garbage, or waiting on us in restaurants. He acknowledged their existence, their effort, thanking them for what they did.

My mother was far less demonstrative and verbal, but taught quiet gratitude. We were reminded constantly, in word and deed, to be aware of what was being done for us, to take nothing for granted. We were taught to distinguish between what we wanted and what we needed, trusting that we would get what we needed, though we could not get all that we wanted. This was simply the reality of life. We were taught to appreciate what we had without comparison with others.

As a parent, I have sought to instill gratefulness in my children. As an educator, I ask myself how I can bring the benefits of gratitude into the classroom. After many years in schools I am aware of how much our educational system, especially at the university level, is based in critical analysis, critical reading, critical writing, and argumentation. We claim that this doesn't mean criticism and argument in the common sense, yet both have a strong tendency to be negative. A student taking one of Stanford's most popular courses exulted, "We learn how to tear apart an article or an idea."

Recognizing my own tendencies of finding faults and dismissing others' ideas, I began to understand how much I was missing, and losing, through this process. Shifting to an appreciative stance, we learn so much more by asking ourselves "What can I learn from this person, this article?" and then discovering that there is always something to learn. From practicing psychotherapy I know the healing and empowering quality of seeing the goodness in people. We can bring to any encounter this same power of viewing others through an appreciative lens.

My colleague Tojo Thatchenkery calls this "appreciative intelligence"[10]—the skill of "seeing the mighty oak in the acorn." You see this ability in creative and successful people who know how to reframe reality to reveal the hidden possibilities within even the most seemingly unpromising situations. People who possess appreciative intelligence are realistic and action-oriented, with the ability not only to identify positive potential but also to devise a course of action for taking advantage of it to achieve good outcomes.

Appreciation is a powerful leadership attribute. If a leader can spread appreciative intelligence throughout a group or organization, it enables all members to become more creative, resilient, successful, and personally fulfilled. Appreciative intelligence is related to appreciative inquiry.[11] This is a search for knowledge designed to help evolve the vision and will of a group or organization. Rather than focusing on fixing problems, appreciative inquiry attempts to create a shared consensus of a new future by exploring and building on the core competencies unique to an organization. Instead of an image of an organization as a problem to be fixed, it is seen as a mystery to be appreciated.

Heartfulness groups develop appreciative intelligence. Those of us in such groups present our stories rather than our arguments, showing appreciation for the genuineness in others' stories. We respond to others' contributions nonjudgmentally, looking for the positive and for points of connection. Rather than competitive, win-lose dialogues in which one individual emerges as the "best," we engage in win-win dialogues, collaboratively moving ahead. Gratitude flows naturally in this heartful community, when it is grounded in vulnerability and humility.

The gratitude that students show circles back to me. In a recent class, a student asked me, "Sensei, what was the best moment in your life?" and I answered without hesitation, "Right now, to be here with you." I was surprised to hear myself say it, and even more astonished to realize that I actually meant it. It gave me a wondrous feeling of peace and dignity. I knew that I was in the right place at that moment. I wanted to be there; I wasn't thinking of great times in the past or indulging in future fantasies. I was mindful of the moment and grateful for the opportunity. This class was a place of peaceful spirit, where I and my students alike could be just as we are, in our original nature—our authentic selves.

Gratitude in Practice

While the roots of adopting gratitude as a good way of living are ancient, its current popularity is actually based on science. Mindfully noticing, appreciating, and enjoying the elements of one's life affects our well-being, and a growing body of evidence shows that gratitude builds psychological, social, and spiritual resources.[12] Recognizing what life gives and offers makes us feel rich and blessed; reminding ourselves of our good fortune in receiving these gifts is a way of overcoming life's trials. A grateful response to life circumstances is an adaptive psychological process by which we positively interpret everyday experiences.

Gratitude is one of the emotions whose roots lie in the capacity to empathize with others and feel our interconnectedness. The experience of gratitude, along with the actions stimulated by it, build and strengthen social relationships. Focusing on the benefits we receive gives us a warm feeling of being loved and cared for, encouraging a desire to give back directly to the givers and to others, as well. When we express our gratitude to others, we strengthen our relationship with them.

Cultivating a way of being based in heartful gratitude is something we all can do. Experience tells us that this is a good way to live. Gratefulness begins with mindful awareness, then we see and listen, opening our hearts for opportunities to help others, too, and inviting ourselves to do something.

Interventions such as writing exercises can be used in daily life to increase gratitude, and consequently to improve wellbeing.[13] These simple interventions showing that gratitude is related to well-being stand in stark contrast to studies showing that huge increases in income are needed for even modest gains in feeling well-being. Research reinforces the spiritual belief that greater peace can be found in learning to appreciate what we have instead of spending our lives desiring more material possessions and achievements. From a scientific view, we can't be sure if gratitude actually causes well-being, but we know intuitively that it is good for us, as well as for others, since the moral and spiritual values of gratitude have often been instilled in us since childhood.

Brother David Steindl-Rast, a Benedictine monk, meditates and writes on how the gentle power of gratefulness makes people happy.[14] He reminds us how awareness of each moment is the most valuable thing that we have, one that gives us the opportunity to do something over and over again, because every moment is a new chance.

Though this makes sense to us, resistance may arise when we are *told* to be grateful, because we feel there is so much suffering in our lives. Yet focusing on gratitude does not mean that we have to be grateful for everything, either on a personal level—for our failures, our injuries, our illnesses—or on a global level—for evils, terrors, and horrors in the world. We do not have to be grateful to everybody: the noisy neighbor, the disrespectful boss, the police officer who treats us unjustly.

We may believe that we should embrace everything in our lives, because it is our fate, karma, or dharma that makes us who we are. Great beauty lies in this way of being. But can most humans be grateful for everything? In many cases, the best we can do is to accept. We may not be able to be grateful for our trauma, but we can accept it and move on with courage.

Gratitude and Society

Science has shown that practicing gratitude increases happiness and health in an individual. Having more healthy individuals in the world is certainly positive. But the importance of teaching gratitude is guided by a belief that the benefits of that attitude for the individual are also transferred to society. My experience in heartful communities is that gratitude springs naturally from the consciousness created by our practices. I find that heartfulness moves us from dissatisfaction, fear, and narcissism to satisfaction, trust, and a deeper appreciation of our interconnectedness. It frees us to live in the present and to accept each moment and every circumstance and each other as gifts. Our discontent with life is broken, and we begin anew in the recognition of what we actually have rather than what we appear to lack.

Steindl-Rast sees gratefulness as a revolutionary force:

> There is a wave of gratefulness because people are becoming aware of how important this is and how it can change our world. Because if you're grateful, you're not fearful, and if you're not fearful, you're not violent. If you're grateful, you act out of a sense of enough and not of a sense of scarcity, and you are willing to share. If you are grateful, you are enjoying the differences between people, and you are respectful to everybody, and that changes this power pyramid under which we live. It doesn't make for equality, but it makes for equal respect, and that is the important thing.[15]

Some people fear that gratitude can be used to oppress, as the oppressor's message is that "you should be grateful for what we give you, and not ask for more." But this is not an either/or situation, and I believe that we can be grateful for what we are given *and* can also ask for more, for full equality and justice. I see gratitude as a path toward rejection of the "scarcity" way of thinking, or the way of seeing the need to hoard and fear the other. A synergy paradigm sees abundance and sharing as ways to peace.

A heartful path to gratefulness consists of vulnerability and authenticity, accepting our imperfection and incompleteness. The sense of peace that arises with gratitude comes from accepting the reality that we can't manage alone, that we do not have to strive to be superhuman. Even if we are not so brilliant, not so perfect, we are just fine as we are.

We challenge ourselves to see the difficulties given to us by rising to that opportunity, by learning something, like patience or standing up for our convictions. So, while there are many things for which we can't be grateful, we can still try to cultivate gratefulness for even difficult moments, because we have the opportunity to do something.

Rather than the habitual way of rushing through life not seeing these chances, there is always the possibility of being grateful in every given moment for the opportunities that are given to us, to use them to make something out of life. When we fail—and we *will* fail—we get another opportunity. We always get another opportunity, and that's the wonderful richness of life and the source of continual hope. And yet another reason to be grateful.

The way of *Bushido* teaches me appreciation for the gift of life. We can contemplate death, take nothing for granted, and come alive with gratitude. Being awake and aware of the mystery and wonder of each moment, being conscious of my connection to nature and all other beings and forces in the universe, fills me with appreciation and lets me cultivate a grateful heart.

This can be a habit, a practice of daily life.

I am learning to live with the mantra *"This is as good as it gets."* It brings me to the peaceful realization that being where I am right now has to be appreciated, moment by moment.

This awareness brings a wonderful sense that I am right where I am, enabling me not to think of the past or to worry about the future, just being mindful of being in the moment, and grateful to be there.

EXERCISES

I. Journal Your Gratitude

1. Get a notebook to keep by your bed, and call it your gratitude journal.
2. Every night before you go to sleep, write down 5 things for which you are grateful on that day. Write things about yourself, other people in your life, situations, or experiences.
3. Do this for at least one week and notice how it makes you feel.

    Go here for hints on how to keep the journal:

    https://greatergood.berkeley.edu/article/item/tips_for_keeping_a_gratitude_journal.

II. Express Thanks

We often feel bad about not thanking people for what they have done for us. Take the simple action of thanking someone who has done something for you.

1. Call to mind someone who did something for you for which you are extremely grateful but to whom you never expressed your deep gratitude. This could be a relative, friend, teacher, or colleague. Try to pick someone who is still alive and could meet you face-to-face. You might select a person that you haven't thought about for a while.
2. Write a short letter to that person as though you were addressing them directly. Describe what this person did, why you are grateful, and how their behavior affected your life. Describe what you are doing in your life now and how you remember his or her efforts.
3. The optional next step is to deliver the letter, if possible. Or you might deliver the same message by phone or video chat.

8

SERVICE

As a human being I acknowledge that my well-being depends on others, and caring for others' wellbeing is a moral responsibility I take seriously. It's unrealistic to think that the future of humanity can be achieved on the basis of prayer or good wishes alone; what we need is to take action. Therefore, my first commitment is to contribute to human happiness as best I can.[1]
—THE DALAI LAMA

When we realized that she could no longer live alone in Japan, we brought Grandmother to the United States to spend her last years. After all, she was 99, and how long could she possibly live? Better to die among those she loved the most, we reasoned. She could pass her remaining time in peace and would be able to die surrounded by her only child and her grandchildren.

Since she had never lived in America, we decided it would be best to have a trial and tell her that she could return to Japan if she decided that it was the best thing to do. But since she could no longer live alone, should she decide to go back, she would have to enter a nursing home. I escorted her from her home in Matsuyama and she moved in with my mother and older sister in Massachusetts. I returned to Tokyo.

Days passed and tensions mounted. As the time approached for a decision to be made, I received a phone call from my older sister, who does not speak Japanese, requesting that I ask Grandmother what she wanted to do.

"Okay," I said, and when the phone was passed, asked, "What do you want to do, Grandma?"

"I think I should go back."

She gave the phone to my sister and I translated into English.

"She thinks she should go back."

This answer did not satisfy my sister, who insisted, "I want to know what *she* wants to do, not what she thinks she should do."

"Okay, I'll ask her again."

"Big sister wants to know what *you* want to do, Grandma."

"Well, I think your mother wants me to go back."

I translated this, too.

My sister said, "That might be true but I want to know what *she* wants to do."

"Okay, I'll try again."

"Grandma, don't worry about what you think Mom wants, what do *you* want to do?"

"I think your sister's husband is not comfortable with me here."

I told her, and my sister said, "Tom's fine with whatever we decide. What does *she* want to do?"

"Sister says her husband is fine with you here. She wants to know what *you* want to do."

"It's probably better for everyone if I go back."

My sister was getting a little frustrated. "I'm not asking her that. I want to know what *she* wants. Tell her that if she wants to stay, I will take care of her."

"Big sister says if you want to stay she will take care of you."

"I appreciate it, but I should probably go back."

"She thinks she should go back," I told my sister, realizing we were back where we started.

She replied, "I just want to know what *she* wants to do."

I was getting exasperated, and said, "I know you do, but maybe she just can't answer your question in the way you want her to."

There was a silence, then my sister said, "Okay, I understand."

Loyalty

Grandmother went back to Japan a month later, after only three months living in America. She moved into a nursing home without complaint. She lived there for 12 years until she died at 111. Would she have been happier in the United States? We don't know, though we feel sad and imagine that she was lonely living that way. It was her choice, I say to myself. But what does this mean for her to choose what she wanted—a woman raised at a time and place in which a woman's desires did not matter, raised in a society in which she could only see herself in a contextual web of relationships? When we asked her "What do *you* want to do?," could she possibly see her wishes simply as personal, individualistic desires?

What Grandmother wanted is what was best for all her loved ones. Japanese culture, even in the language, shows how humans are deeply connected to others. The word for self, *Jibun,* consists of two *kanji,* 自分, together showing how the self is part of something larger. Thinking of my grandmother always reminds me that I am connected to others in a network that includes family, friends, and community.

Coming from a samurai family, she was, of course, influenced by the ethics of *Bushido*. People today dismiss *Bushido* as old-fashioned, and in many ways it is, yet it has noble virtues that can be applied to living well, even now. In the moral principle of *chugi,* or loyalty, the interests of the family and of its members were one and inseparable. In author Inazo Nitobe's words: "This interest is bound up with affection—natural, instinctive, irresistible; we can die for one we love with natural love. It is the opposite of individualism which puts self-interest first, seeing one's own pain, pleasure and existence as our greatest concern."[2]

The virtues of service are laid out in *Hagakure,* a manual of *Bushido* dating from the 1700s.[3] *Bushido* stressed that human relations should always be guided by a sense of service to others, and to the samurai this meant service to the master. For people today, this can mean service to our family, our community, our work.

In *Hagakure* we see how *Bushido* regarded authentic communication with colleagues as an act of compassion that can enhance their development: "To give a person one's opinion and correct his faults is an important thing. It is compassionate and comes first in matters of service."

This is a clear expression of heartfulness, connecting mindfulness with compassion and responsibility. Samurai practiced mindfulness long before it was popularized in the West, and employed a style of communication that valued vulnerability, listening, acceptance, and authenticity.

Although its expression varies culturally, seeking a cause beyond ourselves is an intrinsic human need. It might be large, like family, country, religion, or it might be small, like a project, a garden, or a pet. We give our lives meaning by ascribing value to our chosen cause and seeing it as worth sacrificing for. Loyalty also enhances our quality of life, especially for those of us struggling to find meaning in our existence in illness or aging. It may not make us happy, and it may even be painful, but it satisfies our need to give ourselves to something greater than our individual selves and helps make our lives more endurable.

My grandmother expressed virtues of service and loyalty in deciding to sacrifice what she may have felt were her own individual desires for the greater good of all in the family. Seeing the hardship that it would impose on everyone, she determined that the best course of action was to leave the warm nest of family affection and retire to the group home in Japan. Perhaps she considered her sacrifice and death as meaningful when she saw herself as part of something greater—in this case, a family. Grandmother may not have been happy in the sense of having individual desires met, but she may have felt her life was meaningful, for she was contributing to the happiness of others who loved her but could only care for her at great personal expense of time and money.

I used to tease Grandmother by saying she was selfish, because she was always giving and never gave me the chance to be the one giving. My mother taught me that we could find fulfillment in connecting obligation and love by performing our duties to the best of our ability. She expressed this sense of purpose with the words *giri* and *ninjo*. *Giri* is an ancient concept that was once considered a great traditional Japanese cultural value. But to young people today it is regarded as a burden, something that forces the individual to sacrifice himself for the needs of the other. People in Japan in contemporary times may feel oppressed by having to show loyalty to the group, yet the principle still guides their way of living as good citizens, encouraging them to sacrifice their individualistic desires for the greater good.

My mother made sense of Grandmother's decision as one influenced by both *giri* and *ninjo*. *Ninjo* means human feeling. *Ninjo* is usually separated from *giri* as if the two are distinct and conflicting and a person must choose one or the other. By putting the two words together, my mother was telling me that true *giri* was inseparable from *ninjo,* as human feeling, service, and responsibility go together; connecting them was the way to acting responsibly. The *kanji* reveal that there is no heart in *giri,* but there is in *ninjo,* 人情. Grandmother's decision was heartful—both compassionate and responsible.

This way of compassionate giving is promoted by spiritual teachings in many cultures, such as in the Bible, which tells us that giving is a two-way street: *"A man who is kind benefits himself."*[4] The Dalai Lama reminds us that the benefits of connecting compassionately with others come to both receiver and giver: "If you want others to be happy, practice compassion. If you want to be happy, practice compassion."[5]

These teachings are supported by scientific studies showing that acts designed to improve the well-being of others will lead to greater happiness for givers, as well.[6] Psychology research tells us that one of the best ways to enhance our health is to actively contribute to the lives of those around us. Well-being increases more when these acts are associated with concretely framed goals as opposed to abstractly framed ones—despite many people's intuitions to the contrary. This supports spiritual teachings and lessons drawn from mindfulness that it is the small things, the daily opportunities for little acts of kindness, that bring us happiness, not the achievement of big goals or desires.

While loving persons don't give love for selfish reasons, they still receive that which is given back to them. Giving makes the other person a giver also, and both share in the joy of what they have created.

Responsibility

We desire meaning and purpose, and we find it in connecting to something greater than ourselves. We also find it in small ways of making a difference in someone's life.

In my family, service was taught as a virtue; we children needed to respond to the best of our ability to what we were called to do. For me this was framed as doing something to relieve suffering in the world. Because I had been given much, I needed to give back. I was told that I could find purpose and meaning in acting to relieve suffering.

Responsibility has always invoked fear. When I ask myself what life is calling on me to do, the answer can be profoundly disturbing, yet answering the calling can be the way I affirm my life. I find that if we are truly compassionate, we cannot escape from responsibility. Although I too often try to run from it, I sense heartfulness when I am responsible, whether in parenting, teaching, counseling, or mentoring.

My parents instilled this value in me from childhood—because I had ability, I had responsibility to give to others. This is how I became a doctor and a teacher. Later in life, my grandmother constantly gave me the message that I had responsibility to my children, my wife, my mother, and society in general. Because I was given much by others, I needed to give back. I give my students the same message—that connecting compassionately with others is a responsibility.

Thanks to the teachings of my elders, a sense of responsibility is something that has always guided me. When I first went to Harvard, it was with a sense of mission to be a bridge between East and West, Japan and the United States. This kept me on the right path, as I encountered temptations that were part of the socialization into an elite profession at a prestigious university. I tried to make choices that kept me on this path to achieve my mission, including dedicating years to learning the Japanese language and culture. When many classmates were choosing Harvard hospitals for their training, I selected an unpaid, community-based internship in San Francisco to work with Asian-Americans.

Various circumstances in my life, including racial trauma, have given me a sense of difference, isolation, even alienation that I have battled. I have always had a sense of marginality, a feeling of being an outsider, a stranger. There has been a cost; I have struggled with bonding, belonging, and believing. Too often I wallow in victimization rather than claiming my agency. But this struggle has given me a passion that I have turned into a mission. Knowing discrimination has given me love for the oppressed, an intolerance of injustice.

My career has brought me satisfaction and meaning, as I know that my work has benefited many people. However, I also know that my good work has always been balanced by my desire to indulge in privilege. I have lived well—not extravagantly, but comfortably. I have benefited from and bought into a system that rewards me and encourages belief in the myth of meritocracy. To maintain my balance, I rely on experiences that teach me humility and help me avoid the defenses of arrogance—reductionism, ridicule, denial of confusion, and pride.

The more we enter into the world of power, privilege, and elitism, the more the temptations grow. At the Stanford graduation ceremony, there is a moment when the president of the university bestows on all graduates the "rights, responsibilities, and privileges associated with a degree granted by Stanford University." When he says the word "privileges," the students shout out in unison with him. Though they are having fun, this moment always disturbs me, because I feel that they are showing how much they value their "privileges" over rights and responsibilities. For me, "rights" are crucial to safeguard for themselves and others. And "responsibilities" are the way they will put their values into action through service to society as good citizens.

So, I was glad, one year, when the president addressed this issue directly in his message to graduates shortly after awarding them their degrees, telling them that the rights and privileges of education bring a responsibility to make good use of their knowledge, to change the world for the better, and to help ensure that succeeding generations have the same opportunities they have had at Stanford. Despite what happens at the graduation ceremony, I have had many students who recognize that their newfound freedom comes with responsibilities.

Living Free of Fear

The poet and writer Audre Lorde teaches us that our vision, our goal, our purpose, even our mission are all crucial in overcoming fear. "When I dare to be powerful, to use my strength in the service of my vision, then it becomes less and less important whether I am afraid."[7] Sometimes we glimpse the power that is in all of us, sensing that if we can let this light shine, it gives others freedom to do the same, and knowing that liberating ourselves from our own fear liberates others.

Fear holds us back from having the courage to follow our heart. Fear of failure, responsibility, or even our own greatness inhibits our efforts, impelling us toward mediocrity and safety. Fear stops us from acting responsibly, keeping us stuck in passivity and victimization, unable to change. The *kanji* for fear, 恐, shows a leaking heart, for fear drains our spirit.

Awareness of one's abilities and purpose fosters responsibility to act. This requires courage. The hope is that if we *do* act, the benefits of our actions will spread to others. But where do we get this courage and hope?

Gandhi encourages us to begin with personal change, as it has the power to affect social change:

> If we could change ourselves, the tendencies in the world would also change. As a man changes his own nature, so does the attitude of the world change towards him.... We need not wait to see what others do.[8]

In heartfulness, we overcome fear and our nature changes by mindfully focusing our energies on our connectedness with others, thus awakening compassion. We are willing to do certain things because the welfare of others is our concern. The philosopher Cornel West draws a connection between love and responsibility:

> When you love people, you hate the fact that they're being treated unfairly. You tell the truth. You sacrifice your popularity for integrity. There is a willingness to give your life back to the people

given that, in the end, they basically gave it to you, because we are who we are because somebody loved us anyway.[9]

Today responsibility is often meant to denote duty, something imposed on one from the outside. But responsibility, in its true sense, is an entirely voluntary act, a response to the needs, expressed or unexpressed, of another human being. Erich Fromm reminds us that to be "responsible" means to be able to and ready to "respond" and is an element of love.

Some people think that there is a contradiction between freedom and responsibility. Even the bonds between family members are often considered a burden. When we are so concerned with enjoying our individual freedoms, responsibility can be seen as what keeps us from actually doing so.

john powell helps us to understand that justice involves claiming a shared, common humanity; there is true freedom to be found in our connectedness. Our individualistic society idealizes our autonomy, but we need to embrace our interdependency:

Freedom is found not in autonomy but in embeddedness. To be free is to have access to many interdependent relationships. The more communities one has access to the more options one has for living a full and meaningful life. Inclusivity brings security.[10]

In heartfulness, our connectedness gives us concern for the life and the growth of that which we love. We respond with compassion, sensing that the lives of our brothers and sisters are not their concern alone, but ours, too. We feel responsible for our fellow humans, as we do for ourselves. When we respond with love, our acts are not a burden or a sacrifice; they are simply an expression of our morals and values.

Service and Leadership

A sense of service can be learned by engaging in leadership training that connects personal with political as well as self-reflection with social responsibility. One form is public narrative, as developed by the social activist and professor Marshall Ganz,

who was inspired by the words of Rabbi Hillel:
> If I am not for me, who will be?
> If I am only for me, what am I?
> If not now, when?[11]

In public narrative we learn to tell stories of how we are called to serve. Stories communicate our values through the language of the heart. What we feel inspires us and others with the courage to act. We use both the "head" and the "heart" to mobilize others to act effectively.

Servant leadership is another form of action that embodies a sense of being called to serve. The servant leader shares power, puts the needs of others first, and helps people to be healthy, wise, and free. This kind of leader realizes that an organization exists in a complex educational, social, economic, and governmental ecosystem. They feel responsible not only to stockholders, but also to employees, customers, vendors, and the community at large. Many religious teachings call for a style of servant leadership.

These concepts of leadership are radically changing our views of leaders. Grace Lee Boggs points out that "leader" implies "follower," and asserts that we need to embrace the idea that "we are the leaders we've been looking for." Boggs gives us the clear message that we all have a responsibility to assume leadership. She encourages us with the words of Martin Luther King, Jr.: "To view love and compassion not as some sentimental weakness but as the key that somehow unlocks the door which leads to ultimate reality."[12]

Her mission is to nurture the transformational leadership capacities of individuals and organizations committed to creating productive, sustainable, ecologically responsible, and just communities. Through local, national, and international networks of activists, artists, and intellectuals, she and her colleagues foster new ways of living, being, and thinking to face the challenges of the 21st century. Despite the immensity of the problems facing us, Boggs places importance on such basic things as growing gardens:

The importance of inner-city gardens is not just bringing healthy food to people denied it, but a different way of relating to time and history and to the earth. A garden helps young people relate to the earth in a different way. It helps them to relate to their elders in a different way. It helps them to relate to time in a different way.... If you just press a button and you think that's the key to reality, you're in a hell of a mess as a human being.[13]

Boggs devoted years of her life to active engagement in social justice issues, encouraging her followers to embrace the power within us to change our reality. A major barrier to engagement is victim consciousness. We cling to our identity as victims, though we sense that we are stuck in our development, denying ourselves growth and maturity. Blaming someone for our misfortune is ultimately self-defeating and does not allow us to rise above the situation and to move on with our healing. If we haven't forgiven, we keep creating an identity around our pain.

We need compassion and loving-kindness to avoid resentments and hatred, and to understand suffering in the world—our own and others. This is done through social responsibility. Engaging in the work to alleviate suffering, we recognize how spiritual work may lead to social justice work.

As john powell writes:

> Highly attuned seekers and leaders have the ability to see across categories and bring love into even the most difficult situations. They place themselves in service to more than caring for those in pain. They place themselves in service to the public face of love: justice.[14]

Spirituality and Social Responsibility

Service is related to responsibility, which is an active form of loving as expressed through giving to the world. Loving persons give of themselves, the most precious gift they have. In service, they give what is alive in them—their joy, their knowledge, their humor, their sadness. For the playwright George Bernard Shaw, the calling to serve others is "true joy itself."[15] Psychologist William James describes the calling as "a sort of deep enthusiastic bliss, of bitter willingness to do and suffer anything."[16] While joy and bliss are welcomed by most people, suffering is not easily embraced. These calls to follow ideals are noble, but in reality most people choose the easier path. Those who choose the more difficult path are often guided by their sense of authenticity, passion, and, sometimes even more, a sense of mission.

Dag Hammarskjold, a former Secretary-General of the United Nations, engaged in an intense spiritual struggle in the heat of his professional life and amid his most exacting responsibilities for keeping world peace. He wrote of finding inspiration for service in the writing of mystics for whom self-surrender was the way to self-realization. They followed the call of duty in responding to the needs of their community:

> We are not permitted to choose the frame of our destiny. But what we put into it is ours. He who wills adventure will experience it—according to the measure of his courage. He who wills sacrifice will be sacrificed—according to the measure of his purity of heart.[17]

Hammarskjold sacrificed his life when his plane crashed in Congo on a peacekeeping mission, possibly shot down by those opposed to his intervention. For others, the sacrifice is less extreme but still profound. The psychologist Erik Erikson wrote of how revolutionary writers from national or ethnic minority groups are often both artistic spokespeople as well as prophets of identity confusion:

> These martyrs of self-chosen or accidentally aggravated identity consciousness sacrifice the innocent unity of living to a revolutionary awareness.... The preoccupation with identity may be seen not only as a symptom of alienation but also as a corrective trend in psychosocial evolution.[18]

This kind of artistic creation includes a moral decision that a certain painful identity consciousness may have to be tolerated by artists. This is required for them to provide others with the insights necessary to heal themselves of what most deeply divides and threatens them. These artists are fulfilling a responsibility to help us fellow humans overcome our destructive way of dividing into "us" and "them," by realizing our oneness.

I often ask myself what this talk about service as responsibility and sacrifice means to my young students. I wonder if it is responsible to encourage them to have ideals, to sacrifice. I question if I am raising false hopes. Looking at the world I live in, it seems that idealism is only for the heroes, while the rest of us are resigned to mediocrity. The price of sanity is apparently accommodating to this world in which we live, with identities as bland as a suburban home. Some colleagues say that our job is to avoid the spiritual and just teach academics. Others say that ideals are merely sources of delusion—that students will only be let down when they realize that living by ideals is impossible. I sense that my responsibility to my students is to encourage them to live a balanced life.

Nevertheless, embracing an ideal of service can produce a unity of being in which you feel clarity about your life and what to do. You feel a sense of purpose, which gives you courage and compassion. You may not live up to these ideals, but you feel more grounded, more balanced, more whole.

We are persistently called to abandon our core values and spiritual practices to embrace the worldly values of efficiency, speed, status, security, greater income, and more material comforts. Most of us cannot abandon this world, so we look for guides who provide us with models for how to go about seeking a life that is spiritual within our demanding worldly context. Such spiritual leaders try to travel a life path that will lead them to a destination where they can fully integrate into their lives the love of God, compassion for others, and unity with men and women of all faiths or no faiths. In living out that destiny, they are examples of people who not only talked the talk but also walked the walk.

In the end, the best I can do is offer ideals to help young people, even older people, to think deeply about their lives and maybe to change them. I use whatever wisdom I have to help create possibilities for living. This is the meaning of dharma as I understand it—the innate characteristic that makes a being what it is and the unique roles that each of us plays in this world. For every one of us, the challenge is to understand our own dharma and to do what is required in the pursuit and execution of our nature and true calling, or purpose, thus playing out our role in this wondrous life.

Heartfulness and Social Action

In recent years, the representation of mindfulness as a thin white, blonde woman, sitting cross-legged with eyes closed, "mindfully" seeking "inner peace" in a beautiful natural setting, is being challenged. Mindfulness is no longer seen as a luxury of the privileged, as something not for common or minority people, who have too many more-basic concerns. People are asserting that it is more than a way of personal gain or corporate growth, and it has the potential to transform self and society.[19]

I offered my first class, called "Heartfulness," at Stanford in 2016. The following year, A-lan Holt, Mark Gonzales, and I offered a new course, "Living Free: Embodying Healing and Creativity in the Era of Racial Justice Movements." Our students and we endeavor to connect mindfulness with diversity and social justice, as well as to foster liberation, personal and interpersonal healing, social action, and inclusive community building. Our heartful practice takes students beyond the level of the intellect and political consciousness to the place of integrating their learning into their very selves.[20] They become more able to engage in the difficult process of confronting the ideologies that produce inequalities in society, acknowledging their own privilege, and learning more equitable and empowering ways of relating to one another. They remain present when difficult topics emerge, rather than distancing themselves from situations that are ripe with potential for learning.

We could look on this work as simply helping privileged people to feel better about enjoying their privilege. As we see mindfulness enter the mainstream areas of elite business entities like Google, or privileged universities like Stanford, or powerful organizations such as the U.S. Navy, we can ask whether the practice really changes anything. Does mindfulness, in fact, help to create a kinder, gentler, more-just world?

The constant talk about happiness, I hope, serves to raise issues such as equality, justice, truth, and ethics. But saying that happiness is an individual choice, that it all depends on our attitude and that circumstances are irrelevant, might normalize inequality and oppression. If our life conditions don't matter, and if we can all be equally happy, then feeling happy can provide a convenient excuse to stop dismantling structural barriers like class, social and economic inequality, or poverty. Heartfulness addresses these sinister illusions by actively and explicitly connecting mindfulness with a greater good through compassion and responsibility.

People who care about transforming self are coming together with others who care about transforming society. In January 2015, Jon Kabat-Zinn engaged in a dialogue with scholar Angela Davis, on the topic of "Mindfulness and the Possibility of Freedom."[21] Davis challenged Kabat-Zinn about the meaning of mindfulness in society with a series of questions, including the following: In a racially unjust world, what good is mindfulness? Does it serve the privileged? Is mindfulness a way of enabling people to fully participate in the frantic pace of the capitalist game while sustaining the perception that they are not really in it? Can mindfulness genuinely support social justice?

Kabat-Zinn responded with his belief that the heightened awareness enabled by mindfulness practice can progressively uproot the greed, hatred, and delusion that cause so much collective suffering. Davis countered that racism or sexism are not simply personal attitudes, but instead constitute a whole system of oppression, and questioned whether practices focused on personal habits of mind can generate lasting systemic change. She sees mindfulness as potentially becoming a revolutionary force if embedded in social movements that target oppressive systems, asking what forms that integration would take.

The discussion between Davis and Kabat-Zinn symbolizes the current developments in the integration of mindfulness and social justice. More and more organizations are recognizing the message of heartfulness, and are connecting mindfulness with compassion and responsibility, by helping their members find a sense of purpose in service. They are enabling their members to live more balanced lives, integrating work and family, feeling connected to something greater than their individual selves, and striving to make a difference in the lives of others.

More participants in mindful communities are recognizing their need for diversity and inclusion by engaging in efforts to avoid "spiritual bypassing." Organizations are engaging in the inner work of self-reflection on power and privilege to avoid re-creating structures of injustice in their daily interactions and communities.

Progressive organizations are acknowledging that they need to make a deep and abiding commitment to embody the revolutionary change they seek by employing mindful self-care. Various organizations have begun integrating embodied awareness and mindfulness practices, bridging the inner and outer lives of social change agents, activists, and allies, to support a more effective, more sustainable movement of justice for all. This enables a deeper incorporation of egalitarian values than is possible through solely intellectual exercises, like disseminating information, analyzing, and debating. Heartfulness can also help all of us notice prejudiced thoughts as we become more aware of self and others. If we can be present with our fears, we may confront and overcome barriers to our development, healing wounds to our dignity inflicted by individuals and systems of domination.[22]

The intersection of personal and political transformation is ripe with potential. Mindfulness alone will not spark a political revolution but, when joined by social action, it *will* expand the possibilities for freedom. Each of us can contribute to this movement in which hope defeats despair by taking responsibility, becoming the leader we are searching for—serving by enabling others to achieve purpose in the face of uncertainty.

Heartfulness connects mindfulness and social justice, supporting people in becoming compassionate and responsible members of a community that is just and fair to all its citizens. Embracing leadership, taking responsibility, and engaging with others all require overcoming our feelings of helplessness in the face of life's seemingly overwhelming demands. We may ask ourselves how we can be happy when so many others suffer. But whenever we feel that we can't go on, we may realize that we must move on in trying to solve the world's intolerable problems of hunger, war, pollution, and injustice. We move on to avoid becoming trapped in a wasteland of consumerism or sinking into the fog of depression or the numbness of alcohol, drugs, sex, or violence.

We may already be acting with compassion toward people familiar to us and the ground we live on; we may be teaching our children, listening to our friends, tending our gardens. This book encourages another kind of compassionate action, toward those who are calling from a distance in pain, and whose voices are reaching us. Our individual caring responses are needed, as are programs that address, prevent, and correct suffering, injustice, and inequality. Ram Dass and Mirabai Bush remind us that "When we hear the cry, in order to continue to live honestly with ourselves and others, we want to respond, and that response may bring some of us closer together and eliminate a part of the world's pain."[23]

We may be naive in imagining a better world, knowing that the immense problems of humanity can be resolved only by the participation and initiative of large numbers of people as well as by profound cultural change. The challenge of living is to coexist with such immense problems that lack clear solutions. If we choose not to ignore these difficulties, we might fear that they are so big that our puny efforts can make no difference. We may realize that we are not one of those few exceptional individuals who have the capacity to act and to inspire others on a large scale. Yet each of us *can* take a stand by choosing how we want to be, making our mark. We are all afraid, but we can still affirm life by taking a stand with compassionate responsibility. We may be ineffective, and we may lose, but we are affirming a principle, a way of being.

We who practice heartfulness believe in the interconnectedness of all life. As many mystics and visionaries have pointed out, each individual, in some subtle and mysterious way, embodies all people. If we can bring some healing and well-being to our own life, and then give it in service to just one other person's life, that would be a gentle, humble response to the world's injustice, suffering, and pain. Each of us can act, for ourselves, for others, and for the world in which we live.

Much of my work takes place in a university, where I bring together small groups of students in an effort to help them become more human. It may not seem like much, in the face of the seemingly overwhelming suffering of people and our planet, but it's what I can do. After working with many young people who find it a struggle to be alive and often difficult to empathize with others, I feel heartened by what one student wrote of heartfulness:

> What happens in this class is a kind of tiny miracle. We cross borders, inside ourselves and between us and others, finding the connections that we hunger for and realize that's what we need to keep going. We're filled with gratitude for each other and just for being here.

We stand at a moment that clearly calls for using beginner's mind in sensing the infinite possibilities that exist. We are alive in this strange moment in which humanity teeters on the edge of destruction, while normalizing it all as business as usual. Yet, we move on. What is the meaning in writing a book on mindfulness and heartfulness in these times? I am certainly a fool to believe that it makes any difference. Still, I write on. But isn't this life for most of us? When we think we can't go on, we do move on. This is how we find meaning in life. We do our best with what we've got. This is *my* best. Thank you for reading and caring.

EXERCISES

I. What Is My Purpose?

1. Reflect on the question "What is it that if I don't do it, it probably won't get done?"
2. Write down your thoughts for 10 minutes.
3. Reflect on this statement: "The purpose of life is to do your best with what you've got."
4. Write down your thoughts for 10 minutes.

II. Realizing My Vision

Reflect on Audre Lorde's words: "When I dare to be powerful, to use my strength in the service of my vision, then it becomes less and less important whether I am afraid."

1. Think of something that you want to see happen or realized that depends on your own actions.
2. What holds you back from doing it?

3. Imagine yourself overcoming your fear and acting in service of realizing your vision.
4. Write down your thoughts for 10 minutes.

Notes

Preface

[1] Jerry Garcia and Robert Hunter, "Ripple" (recorded by the Grateful Dead), on *American Beauty* (LP) (Burbank, CA: Warner, 1970).

Introduction

[1] Jon Kabat-Zinn, *Full Catastrophe Living* (New York: Bantam Books, 2013), xxxv.
[2] Chogyam Trungpa, *The Myth of Freedom and the Way of Meditation* (Boulder, CO: Shambhala, 2005).
[3] B. Alan Wallace, Getting Mindfulness Right, https://psychcentral.com/blog/archives/2016/11/15/getting-mindfulness-rightexpert-b-allan-wallace-explains-where-we-are-going-wrong/.
[4] Jon Kabat-Zinn, *Wherever You Go, There You Are: Mindfulness Meditation in Everyday Life* (New York: Hyperion, 1994), 7.

[5] Bill Moyers Journal: Grace Lee Boggs, https://vimeo.com/33217407.

[6] S. Murphy-Shigematsu, How to Help Diverse Students Find Common Ground, http://greatergood.berkeley.edu/article/item/how_to_help_diverse_students_find_common_ground.

Chapter 1

[1] Shunryu Suzuki, *Zen Mind, Beginner's Mind: Informal Talks on Zen Meditation and Practice* (Boulder, CO: Shambhala Publications, 2011).

[2] Mindfulness Training Increases Attention in Children, https://www.sciencedaily.com/releases/2013/09/130905202847.htm.

[3] C. Otto Scharmer, *Theory U: Leading from the Future as It Emerges: The Social Technology of Presencing* (Cambridge, MA: Society for Organizational Learning, 2007).

[4] Daniel Goleman, *Emotional Intelligence: Why It Can Matter*

More Than IQ for Character, Health, and Lifelong Achievement (New York: Bantam, 1995).

[5] bell hooks Urges "Radical Openness" in Teaching, Learning, http://www.ncte.org/magazine/archives/117638.

[6] Valerie Malhotra Bentz and Jeremy J. Shapiro, *Mindful Inquiry in Social Research* (Thousand Oaks, CA: 1998).

[7] Parker J. Palmer and Arthur Zajonc, *The Heart of Higher Education: A Call to Renewal* (San Francisco: Jossey-Bass, 2010).

[8] Dan Barbezat and Mirabai Bush, *Contemplative Practices in Higher Education* (San Francisco: Jossey-Bass, 2014).

[9] Emily Campbell, Research Round-up: Mindfulness in Schools, https://greatergood.berkeley.edu/article/item/research_round_up_school_based_mindfulness_programs.

[10] Chase Davenport and Francesco Pagnini, Mindful Learning: A Case Study of Langerian

Mindfulness in Schools, https://www.ncbi.nlm.nih.gov/pmc/articles/PMC5018476/.
[11] Palmer and Zajonc, *Heart of Higher Education*.
[12] Jon Kabat-Zinn, *Full Catastrophe Living* (New York: Bantam Books, 2013), xxxv.
[13] Wayne Muller, *A Life of Being, Having, and Doing Enough* (San Jose, CA: Harmony, 2011).
[14] John Lennon, "Beautiful Boy (Darling Boy)" (recorded by John Lennon), on *Double Fantasy* (LP) (New York: The Hit Factory, 1980).
[15] Myla and Jon Kabat-Zinn, *Everyday Blessings: The Inner Work of Mindful Parenting.* (New York: Hachette, 1994).
[16] Kahlil Gibran, *The Prophet* (New York: Alfred A. Knopf, 1973).
[17] Daniel Goleman, Richard Boyatzis, and Annie McKee, *Primal Leadership* (Boston: Harvard Business Review Press, 2013).
[18] Edgar H. Schein, *Humble Inquiry: The Gentle Art of*

Asking Instead of Telling (Oakland, CA: Berrett-Koehler, 2013); Scharmer, *Theory U;* Tim Brown, *Change by Design* (New York: HarperCollins, 2009).

[19] Tania Singer and Matthieu Ricard, eds., *Caring Economics: Conversations on Altruism and Compassion, between Scientists, Economists, and the Dalai Lama* (New York: Picador, 2017).

Chapter 2

[1] Tokugawa Ieyasu on Coping with Challenges in Life, Han of Harmony, http://hanofharmony.com/tokugawa-ieyasu-on-copingwith-challenges-in-life/.
[2] Ibid.
[3] Richard Katz and Stephen Murphy-Shigematsu, *Synergy, Healing, and Empowerment: Insights from Cultural Diversity* (Calgary, Can.: Brush Education Inc., 2012).
[4] Ibid.

[5] Chester Pierce, "Offensive Mechanisms," in *The Black Seventies,* Floyd Barbour, ed. (Boston: Porter Sargent Pub., 1970).

[6] Melanie Tervalon, "Cultural Humility versus Cultural Competence: A Critical Distinction in Defining Physician Training Outcomes in Multicultural Education," *Journal of Health Care for the Poor and Underserved* 9, no.2 (1998): 117–25.

[7] Leonard Bernstein, Lehren and Lernen, Teaching and Learning, https://www.youtube.com/watch?v=wwcFdAu0thE.

[8] Tenelle Porter, http://www.slate.com/bigideas/what-do-we-know/essays-and-opinions/tenelle-porter-opinion; Victor Ottati, Erika D. Price, Chase Wilson, and Nathanael Smaktoyo, "When Self-Perceptions of Expertise Increase Closed-Minded Cognition: The Earned Dogmatism Effect," *Journal of*

Experimental Social Psychology 61 (November 2015): 131–38.
[9] bell hooks, http://www.ncte.org/magazine/archives/117638.

Chapter 3

[1] Audre Lorde, *Sister Outsider: Essays and Speeches* (Toronto, ON: Crossing Press, 2007).
[2] bell hooks, *Talking Back: Thinking Feminist, Thinking Black* (New York: South End Press, 1989).
[3] Erik H. Erikson, "The Concept of Identity in Race Relations: Notes and Queries," *Daedulus,* 95:1 (Winter 1966): 151.
[4] Albert Einstein, The World as I See It, https://archive.org/stream/AlbertEinsteinTheWorldAsISeeIt/The_World_as_I_See_it-AlbertEinsteinUpByTj_djvu.txt
[5] How the Brain Changes When You Meditate, https://www.mindful.org/how-the-brain-changes-when-you-meditate/.

[6] Henry James, ed., *The Letters of William James,* vol.1 (Boston: Atlantic Monthly Press, 1920).

[7] "You've got to find what you love," Jobs says, http://news.stanford.edu/2005/06/14/jobs-061505/.

[8] john a. powell, *Racing to Justice: Transforming Our Conceptions of Self and Other to Build an Inclusive Society* (Bloomington: Indiana University Press, 2015).

[9] *Hajimete jibun de jibun o hometai to omoimasu* [The first time I feel like I want to praise myself], http://london2012.nikkansports.com/column/quotations/archives/f-cl-tp0-20120706-978771.html.

[10] Scott Barry Kaufman, "The Differences Between Happiness and Meaning in Life," *Scientific American,* https://blogs.scientificamerican.com/beautiful-minds/the-differences-between-happiness-andmeaning-in-life/.

[11] Roy J. Baumeister, *Meanings of Life* (New York: Guilford Press, 1992).

[12] Emily Esfahani Smith and Jennifer Aaker, In 2017 Pursue Meaning Instead of Happiness, *Science of Us,* http://nymag.com/scienceofus/2016/12/in-2017-pursue-meaning-instead-of-happiness.html.

[13] Nick Craig and Scott A. Snook, "From Purpose to Impact," *Harvard Business Review,* https://hbr.org/2014/05/from-purpose-to-impact.

[14] Derek Beres, Yoga Myths: There Is No Authentic Self, http://upliftconnect.com/no-authentic-self/.

[15] James Pennebaker, "Writing about Emotional Experiences as a Therapeutic Process," *Psychological Science* 8, no.2 (May 1997): 162–66.

[16] James Pennebaker, *Writing to Heal: A Guided Journal for Recovering from Trauma and Emotional Upheaval* (Oakland, CA: New Harbinger Press, 2004).

[17] Todd Kashdan and Robert Biswas-Diener, *The Upside of*

Your Dark Side: Why Being Your Whole Self, not Just Your "Good" Self, Drives Success and Fulfillment (New York: Penguin Publishing, 2015).

[18] Graham Nash, "Teach Your Children" (recorded by Crosby, Stills, Nash, and Young), on *Deja Vu* (LP) (San Francisco: Wally Heider's Studio C, 1970).

[19] Mihaly Csikszentmihalyi, *Creativity: Flow and the Psychology of Discovery and Invention* (New York: Harper Perennial, 2013).

Chapter 4

[1] Three Poems by Pat Parker, http://lithub.com/three-poems-by-patparker/.

[2] Erich Fromm, *The Art of Loving* (New York: Harper, 2006).

[3] Gregory M. Walton, Geoffrey L. Cohen, David Cwir, and Steven J. Spencer, "Mere Belonging: The Power of Social Connections, *Journal of Personal and Social Psychology* 102(3) (March 2012):

513–32, doi: 10.1037/a0025731, epub October 24, 2011.
[4] T.S. Eliot, Little Gidding, http://www.columbia.edu/itc/history/winter/w3206/edit/tseliotlittlegidding.html.
[5] David Desteno, The Kindness Cure, https://www.theatlantic.com/health/archive/2015/07/mindfulness-meditation-empathycompassion/398867/.
[6] Julia Kristeva, *The Kristeva Reader,* trans. Toril Moi (Oxford: Basil Blackwell, 1986).
[7] Albert Einstein, *The World as I See It,* https://archive.org/stream/AlbertEinsteinTheWorldAsISeeIt/The_World_as_I_See_it-AlbertEinsteinUpByTj_djvu.txt.
[8] Three Poems by Pat Parker.
[9] Gloria Anzaldua, "(Un)natural Bridges, (Un)safe Spaces," in *This Bridge We Call Home: Radical Visions for Transformation,* Gloria Anzaldua and AnaLouise Keating, eds. (London: Routledge, 2002).
[10] john a. powell, *Racing to Justice: Transforming Our*

Conceptions of Self and Other to Build an Inclusive Society (Bloomington: Indiana University Press, 2015).
[11] Laurent A. Parks Daloz, "Transformative Learning for the Common Good," in Jack Mezirow and Associates, eds., *Learning as Transformation: Critical Perspectives on a Theory in Progress* (San Francisco: Jossey-Bass, 1991), 103–24.
[12] Anzaldua, "(Un)natural Bridges, (Un)safe Spaces."
[13] Paul Ekman, *Moving Toward Global Compassion* (San Francisco: Paul Ekman Group, 2014).
[14] Dag Hammarskjold, *Markings* (New York: Vintage, 2006).
[15] Mary Field Belenky and Ann V. Stanton, "Inequality, Development, and Connected Knowing," in Jack Mezirow and Associates, eds., *Learning as Transformation: Critical Perspectives on a Theory in*

Progress (San Francisco: Jossey-Bass, 1991), 71–102.
[16] Stephen Murphy-Shigematsu, "Respect and Empathy in Teaching and Learning Cultural Medicine," *Journal of General Internal Medicine* 2010, May 25.
[17] Hirotada Ototake, *Nihon no Tayousei no Genzaichi wa?* [What's the state of Japan's Diversity?], http://www.news-postseven.com/archives/2015070 2_333418.html.

Chapter 5

[1] Thich Nhat Hanh, *Touching Peace* (Berkeley, CA: Parallax Press, 1992).
[2] Shunryu Suzuki, *Zen Mind, Beginner's Mind: Informal Talks on Zen Meditation and Practice* (Boulder, CO: Shambhala Publications, 2011).
[3] Stephen Murphy-Shigematsu, "We Are Not Our Bodies," *Academic Medicine* 84, no.8 (August 2009), 981.

[4] Mimi Guarneri, *The Heart Speaks: A Cardiologist Reveals the Secret Language of Healing* (New York: Touchstone, 2007).

[5] Daniel J. Siegel, *Mindsight: The New Science of Personal Transformation* (New York: Bantam, 2010).

[6] Carl Jung, *Dreams, Memories, and Reflections.* (New York: Vintage, 1965). 134.

[7] Yamamoto Tsunetomo, *Hagakure: The Book of the Samurai,* trans. William Scott Wilson (Tokyo: Kodansha International, 1979).

[8] Carl Rogers and Richard Farson, *Active Listening* (Mansfield Centre, CT: Martino Publishing, 2015).

[9] Amy Chua/Tiger Mom, I didn't expect this level of intensity, https://www.youtube.com/watch?v=GAel_qRfKx8.

[10] Jalal Al-Din Rumi, *The Illuminated Rumi,* trans. Coleman Barks (New York: Broadway Books, 1997).

[11] Henri Nouwen, *Reaching Out: The Three Movements of the*

Spiritual Life (New York: Image, 1986).

[12] Ernest Kurtz and Katherine Ketcham, *The Spirituality of Imperfection: Storytelling and the Search for Meaning* (New York: Bantam, 1993).

[13] Richard Katz and Stephen Murphy-Shigematsu, *Synergy, Healing, and Empowerment: Insights from Cultural Diversity* (Calgary, Can.: Brush Education Inc., 2012).

[14] Edgar Schein, *Humble Inquiry: The Gentle Art of Asking Instead of Telling* (Oakland, CA: Berrett-Koehler, 2013).

[15] Paul J. Zak, Why Your Brain Loves Good Storytelling, https://hbr.org/2014/10/why-your-brain-loves-good-storytelling.

[16] Thich Nhat Hanh, Oprah Winfrey Talks with Thich Nhat Hanh, https://www.youtube.com/watch?v=NJ9UtuWfs3U.

Chapter 6

[1] Jalal Al-Din Rumi, *The Illuminated Rumi,* trans. Coleman Barks (New York: Broadway Books, 1997).

[2] Viktor Frankl, *Man's Search for Meaning* (Boston: Beacon Press, 2006).

[3] Paul Kalanithi, *When Breath Becomes Air* (New York: Random House, 2016).

[4] Kiyo Morimoto, Chapel Talk, unpublished paper, 1984.

[5] His Holiness the Dalai Lama and Howard C. Cutler, *The Art of Happiness* (New York: Riverhead Books, 2009).

[6] Madoka Mayuzumi, *So Happy to See Cherry Blossoms: Haiku from the Year of the Great Earthquake and Tsunami* (Winchester, VA: Red Moon Press, 2014).

[7] Randy A. Sansone and Laurie A. Sansone, Gratitude and Well-Being: The Benefits of Appreciation, https://www.ncbi.nlm.nih.gov/pmc/articles/PMC3010965/.

[8] Todd Kashdan, The Problem with Happiness, http://www.huffingtonpost.com/todd-kashdan/whats-wrong-withhappines_b_740518.html.

[9] Epictetus, Internet Encyclopedia of Philosophy, http://www.iep.utm.edu/epictetu/.

[10] Ram Dass and Mirabai Bush, *Compassion in Action: Setting Out on the Path of Service* (New York: Harmony, 1995).

[11] Jan Thomas, Grace Lee Boggs Sees a Looming Great Sea Change, https://soulandmeaning.com/social-change-spirituality/grace-lee-boggs-sees-a-looming-great-sea-change/.

[12] Shoma Morita, *Morita Therapy and the True Nature of Anxiety-Based Disorders (Shinkeishitsu)* (Albany: State University of New York Press, 1998).

[13] Iris B. Mauss, Maya Tamir, Craig L. Anderson, and Nicole S. Savino, Can Seeking Happiness Make People Unhappy? Paradoxical Effects of

Valuing Happiness, *Emotion* 11(4), 807–15.
[14] Carl Rogers, *On Becoming a Person: A Therapist's View of Psychotherapy* (Wilmington, MA: Mariner Books, 1995).
[15] Richard Katz and Stephen Murphy-Shigematsu, *Synergy, Healing, and Empowerment: Insights from Cultural Diversity* (Calgary, Can.: Brush Education Inc., 2012).
[16] Ecclesiastes 3:1 (King James version).
[17] Mick Jagger and Keith Richards, "You Can't Always Get What You Want" (recorded by the Rolling Stones), on *Let It Bleed* (LP) (London: Olympic Sound Studios, 1968).

Chapter 7

[1] Michelle Obama, transcript of Michelle Obama's Convention Speech, http://www.npr.org/2012/09/04/160578836/transcript-michelle-obamas-convention-speech.

[2] Albert Einstein, Alice Calaprice (ed.), *The Ultimate Quotable Einstein* (Princeton, NJ: Princeton University Press, 2013).

[3] Dalai Lama, Your Precious Human Life, http://buddhistreflections.blogspot.com/2011/01/your-precious-human-life.html.

[4] David K. Reynolds, *The Quiet Therapies: Japanese Pathways to Personal Growth* (Honolulu: University of Hawaii Press, 1983).

[5] Piero Ferrucci, *The Power of Kindness: The Unexpected Benefits of Leading a Compassionate Life* (New York: TarcherPerigee, 2007).

[6] Gregg Krech, *Naikan: Gratitude, Grace, and the Japanese Art of Self-Reflection* (Albany, CA: Stone Bridge Press, 2001).

[7] Anabel Stenzel, *The Power of Two: A Twin Triumph Over Cystic Fibrosis* (Columbia, MO: University of Missouri Press, 2014).

[8] Barnett and Kim Pearce, *Facing West: On Mortality, Compassion,*

and *Moments of Grace* (unpublished journal).

[9] Soh Ozawa, *Nihon no Ki: Fufu Gan no Nikki* [Two Trees: A Couple's Cancer Journal] (Tokyo: NHK Shuppan, 2010).

[10] Tojo Thatchenkery and Carol Metzker, *Appreciative Intelligence: Seeing the Mighty Oak in the Acorn* (San Francisco: Berrett-Koehler Publishers, 2006).

[11] David Cooperrider, What Is Appreciative Inquiry?, http://www.davidcooperrider.com/ai-process/.

[12] Alex M. Wood, Jeffrey J. Froh, and Adam W.A. Geraghty, Gratitude and Well-Being: A Review and Theoretical Integration, https://greatergood.berkeley.edu/pdfs/GratitudePDFs/2Wood-GratitudeWell-BeingReview.pdf.

[13] R.A. Emmons and A. Mishra, "Why Gratitude Enhances Well-Being: What We Know, What We Need to Know," in K. Sheldon, T. Kashdan, and M.F.

Steger, eds., *Designing the Future of Positive Psychology: Taking Stock and Moving Forward* (New York: Oxford University Press, 2012).

[14] David Steindl-Rast, Want to Be Happy? Be Grateful, https://www.ted.com/talks/david_steindl_rast_want_to_be_happy_be_grateful.

[15] Ibid.

Chapter 8

[1] Daniel Goleman, *The Dalai Lama—A Force for Good: The Dalai Lama's Vision for the World* (New York: Bantam Books, 2015), ix.

[2] Inazo Nitobe, *Bushido* (Tokyo: Kodansha International,1998).

[3] Yamamoto Tsunetomo, *Hagakure: The Book of the Samurai,* trans. William Scott Wilson (Tokyo: Kodansha International,1979).

[4] Proverbs 11:17.

[5] Dalai Lama, Twitter, 2:14a.m., December 2010.

[6] Wendy Liu and Jennifer Aaker, "The Happiness of Giving: The Time-Ask Effect," *Journal of Consumer Research* 35, no.3 (2008): 543–57.

[7] Audre Lorde, *The Cancer Journals* (San Francisco: Aunt Lute Books, 1997), 13.

[8] Brian Morton, "Falser Words Were Never Spoken," *New York Times,* August 29, 2011.

[9] Cornel West, *Race Matters* (Boston: Beacon Press, 1993).

[10] john a. powell, *Racing to Justice: Transforming Our Conceptions of Self and Other to Build an Inclusive Society* (Bloomington: Indiana University Press, 2015).

[11] Marshall Ganz, What Is Public Narrative?, https://comm-org.wisc.edu/syllabi/ganz/WhatisPublicNarrative5.19.08.htm.

[12] Grace Lee Boggs, These Are the Times That Try Our Souls, http://animatingdemocracy.org/sites/default/files/documents/reading_room/Grace_Lee_Boggs_Grow_Our_Souls.pdf.

[13] Bill Moyers and Grace Lee Boggs, https://vimeo.com/33217407.
[14] powell, *Racing to Justice.*
[15] George Bernard Shaw, *Man and Superman: A Comedy and a Philosophy,* https://archive.org/stream/manandsupermana06shawgoog#page/n7/mode/2up, 1903, xxxi.
[16] Henry James, ed., *The Letters of William James,* vol.1 (Boston: Atlantic Monthly Press, 1920).
[17] Dag Hammarskjold, *Markings* (New York: Vintage, 2006).
[18] Erik H. Erikson, "The Concept of Identity in Race Relations: Notes and Queries," *Daedulus* 95:1 (Winter 1966): 151.
[19] *The Activist's Ally: Contemplative Tools for Social Change* (Northampton, MA: Center for Contemplative Mind in Society, 2011).
[20] Beth Berila, *Integrating Mindfulness into Anti-Oppression Pedagogy* (New York: Routledge, 2015).

[21] Angela Davis and Jon Kabat-Zinn, Mindfulness and the Possibility of Freedom, https://vimeo.com/117131914.

[22] Angel Kyodo Williams, *Being Black: Zen and the Art of Living with Fearlessness and Grace* (New York: Penguin, 2002).

[23] Ram Dass and Mirabai Bush, *Compassion in Action: Setting Out on the Path of Service* (New York: Harmony, 1995).

Acknowledgments

There are many people I wish to thank for contributing to the creation of this book. A number of them have been mentioned already and their contributions honored. Some have passed on; others remain in my life, and including them in my chapters shows clearly how they have helped me to learn about the art of heartful living.

Many thanks to my students of all ages who have studied with me and taught me, as well.

The staff at Berrett-Koehler has been outstandingly supportive; special thanks to Neal Maillet.

Reviewers of my manuscript were incredibly insightful and instructive; the final product reflects their helpful critiques. James Ong read the manuscript and gave comments that greatly improved the book.

Gratitude to my family, my greatest source of meaning and support, especially to my wife Cheena for sacrificing her own desires and her endless patience, understanding, and trust in the importance of my work.

About the Author

Stephen Murphy-Shigematsu is a psychologist with a doctorate from Harvard University, and with training in clinical and community psychology, yoga, meditation, and Chinese medicine. He was professor of education and psychology at the University of Tokyo and director of the international counseling center. At Stanford University he is cofounder of the LifeWorks program in contemplative and integrative education in the School of Medicine.

Dr. Murphy-Shigematsu has been a teacher and counselor for children and adults in schools and universities in Japan and the United States, from day care to medical school. His work balances traditional wisdom and modern science in designing mindful, gentle, and compassionate educational practices and spaces. He uses storytelling, both written and oral, to enhance whole-person learning and mindful citizenship.

His research career includes fieldwork in Okinawa and other parts of Japan in healing and human development as a Fulbright scholar. His work has contributed to understanding in areas of narrative psychology, mixed-race identity, multicultural counseling, and diversity in Japan as well as the United States. He is also engaged in assessment of mindfulness in promoting personal well-being and social transformation.

At Stanford he teaches a range of heartfulness courses in several programs and departments, including Health and Human Performance and Comparative Studies in Race and Ethnicity, integrating mindfulness, creative expression, and transformative learning.

He develops and teaches similar programs based in heartfulness principles and values for organizations in the United States, including the Marines and the Navy, as well as in Japan and Singapore, in areas of diversity and inclusion, leadership development, and community building. His community work includes leading *Nichibei Care,* an organization promoting mental health in Japanese communities.

The author of books, articles, and blogs in both Japanese and English, Dr. Murphy-Shigematsu writes about multicultural perspectives on mindfulness, identity, and community. His writing, bridging literary and social science genres, is both scholarly and accessible to a wide audience.

He is a co-author of *When Half Is Whole: Multiethnic Asian American Identities* and *Multicultural Encounters: Case Narratives from a Counseling Practice;* and *Synergy, Healing, and Empowerment: Insights from Cultural Diversity.* His books in Japanese include *Amerasian Children: An Unknown Minority Problem;* and *Stanford University Mindfulness Classroom.* He is also the coeditor of *Transcultural Japan: At the Borderlands of Race, Gender, and*

Identity and *Japan's Diversity Dilemmas: Ethnicity, Citizenship, and Education.* For more information on Dr. Murphy-Shigematsu, go to www.murphyshigematsu.com.

Berrett–Koehler
Publishers

Berrett-Koehler is an independent publisher dedicated to an ambitious mission: *Connecting people and ideas to create a world that works for all.*

We believe that the solutions to the world's problems will come from all of us, working at all levels: in our organizations, in our society, and in our own lives. Our BK Business books help people make their organizations more humane, democratic, diverse, and effective (we don't think there's any contradiction there). Our BK Currents books offer pathways to creating a more just, equitable, and sustainable society. Our BK Life books help people create positive change in their lives and align their personal practices with their aspirations for a better world.

All of our books are designed to bring people seeking positive change together around the ideas that empower them to see and shape the world in a new way.

And we strive to practice what we preach. At the core of our approach is

Stewardship, a deep sense of responsibility to administer the company for the benefit of all of our stakeholder groups including authors, customers, employees, investors, service providers, and the communities and environment around us. Everything we do is built around this and our other key values of quality, partnership, inclusion, and sustainability.

This is why we are both a B-Corporation and a California Benefit Corporation—a certification and a for-profit legal status that require us to adhere to the highest standards for corporate, social, and environmental performance.

We are grateful to our readers, authors, and other friends of the company who consider themselves to be part of the BK Community. We hope that you, too, will join us in our mission.

A BK Life Book

BK Life books help people clarify and align their values, aspirations, and actions. Whether you want to manage your time more effectively or uncover your true purpose, these books are designed to instigate infectious positive change that starts with you. Make your mark!

To find out more, visit www.bkconnection.com.

Berrett–Koehler Publishers
Connecting people and ideas
to create a world that works for all

Dear Reader,

Thank you for picking up this book and joining our worldwide community of Berrett-Koehler readers. We share ideas that bring positive change into people's lives, organizations, and society.

To welcome you, we'd like to offer you a free e-book. You can pick from among twelve of our bestselling books by entering the promotional code **BKP92E** here: http://www.bkconnection.com/welcome.

When you claim your free e-book, we'll also send you a copy of our e-newsletter, the *BK Communiqué.* Although you're free to unsubscribe, there are many benefits to sticking around. In every issue of our newsletter you'll find

- A free e-book
- Tips from famous authors
- Discounts on spotlight titles
- Hilarious insider publishing news

- A chance to win a prize for answering a riddle

Best of all, our readers tell us, "Your newsletter is the only one I actually read." So claim your gift today, and please stay in touch!

Sincerely,
Charlotte Ashlock
Steward of the BK Website
Questions? Comments? Contact me at bkcommunity@bkpub.com.

Index

A
acceptance,
  balance, *206, 207*
  change, *219, 220*
  community, *13, 76, 212, 220*
  empathy, *123, 190, 192, 193, 223*
  exercises, *225*
  heartfulness, *192, 198, 200, 207, 208, 211, 212, 213, 217, 219, 220*
  Japanese culture, *193, 195, 197, 198, 200, 202, 204, 206, 207*
  liberation, *193, 204, 206, 207, 208, 211, 212, 213, 215, 217, 219, 220*
  loss, *222, 223*
  maturity, *69, 83, 93, 153, 158*
  resilience, *198, 200, 202, 204, 206*
  suffering, *193, 195, 197*
  victimization, *213, 215*
  vulnerability, *195, 211, 243*
  writing, *202, 204*
African-Americans, *56, 57, 60, 61, 83, 85, 86, 113*
akido, *141*
Alcoholics Anonymous, *181, 234*
Anzaldua, Gloria, *128, 129, 133*
Arima, Hatsuko, *29*
Arimoto, Yuko, *99, 101*
arugamama (unconditional acceptance), *217*
Asian-Americans, *60, 81, 83, 85, 86, 88, 89, 91, 93, 116, 118, 120, 121, 133, 143, 153, 206, 277*
authenticity,
  community, *99, 101, 106, 108, 110, 111, 123, 124*
  doubt, *94, 96*

empathy, *99, 104, 111*
exercises, *113*
heartfulness, *35, 36, 270*
mindfulness, *94, 96*
parenting, *29, 110*
passion, *101, 103, 104, 286*
purpose, *99, 101, 103, 104*
self-acceptance, *88, 89, 91, 93, 94, 110, 111*
vulnerability, *72, 74, 76, 89, 108, 121, 259*
Autobiography of Malcolm X, The (Malcolm X), *85*
'Beautiful Boy' (Lennon), *25*

B
beginner's mind,
　empathy, *52, 63, 89, 211*
　exercises, *38, 39*
　health care, *18, 20, 22, 23, 25*
　heartfulness,

leadership, *30, 32, 34, 35, 36*
mindfulness, *7, 8, 10, 11, 13, 15, 16, 18*
Zen, *1, 5, 7*
Benedict, Saint, *166, 168*
Bernstein, Leonard, *64*
Black Panthers, *85*
Blue Hawaii (Taurog), *81*
Boggs, Grace Lee, *283, 285, 286*
Brown, H. Rap, *85, 86*
Buddhism, *67, 197, 198, 207, 234*
　See also Zen,
Bush, Mirabai, *212, 213, 298*
Bushido, *153, 171, 250, 259, 268, 270*

C
Cambridge, Massachusetts, *3, 5, 20*
Canada, *51*

Christianity, *103, 207, 208, 211, 222, 234, 273*
Chua, Amy, *176*
chugi (loyalty), *268, 270*
connectedness, community, *16, 18, 36, 49, 99, 111, 118, 120, 121, 123, 124, 126, 128, 129, 131, 133, 138, 139, 232, 268, 294, 296, 298, 299, 300*
empathy, *118, 121, 123, 124, 126, 128, 129, 131, 133, 134, 136, 138, 139, 141, 143, 144, 146, 148, 156, 281*
exercises, *150*
gratitude, *233, 234, 255, 256, 258*
heartfulness, *211, 212, 280*
identity, *116, 118, 128, 131, 133, 141, 143, 144*
suffering, *144, 146*
vulnerability, *51, 139*
Csikszentmihalyi, Mihaly, *111*

D
Dalai Lama, *197, 198, 234, 236, 263, 273*
Davis, Angela, *212, 294*
death, *71, 111, 153, 155, 156, 158, 192, 202, 243, 245, 246, 247, 250, 259, 260, 272*
Dharamsala, India, *234*
dharma, *256, 292*
'Duck Syndrome', *61, 63*
dukkha (suffering), *197*
Dweck, Carol, *66, 67*

E
East Asian medicine, *10, 18, 20, 22, 23, 54*
Einstein, Albert, *7, 91, 123, 124, 232, 233*
Eliot, T.S., *121*
Ellison, Ralph,
  Invisible Man, *85*
Epictetus, *208*
Erikson, Erik, *88, 288*

exercises, *38, 39, 78, 113, 150, 187, 225, 262, 302*

F

Frankl, Victor, *192*
Franklin, Aretha, *85*
Freud, Sigmund, *215*
Fromm, Erich, *281*

G

ganbaru (do your best), *198, 200, 202*
Gandhi, Mahatma, *280*
Ganz, Marshall, *283*
Gaye, Marvin, *85*
Gelb, David,
    Jiro Dreams of Sushi, *101*
Gibran, Kahlil, *27*
giri (loyalty to the group), *272, 273*
Goethe, Johann Wolfgang von, *20, 141*
Gonzales, Mark, *292*
gratitude,
    acceptance, *195, 204, 229, 230, 232, 233, 234, 236*
    community, *190, 206, 232, 233, 234, 258, 259, 260*
    empathy, *158, 255*
    exercises, *262*
    forgiveness, *240, 241, 243*
    heartfulness, *230, 240, 241, 243, 252*
    illness, *243, 245, 246, 247, 250*
    leadership, *251, 252*
    parenting, *250, 251*
    practice, *255, 256*
    self-reflection, *236, 238, 240, 241, 243, 245, 246, 247, 250, 251, 252, 255, 256, 258, 259, 260*
    teaching, *250, 251*
Great Hanshin-Awaji Earthquake, Japan (1995), *202, 204*

H

Hagakure (book), *171, 270*
Hammarskjold, Dag, *138, 288*

Harvard University, *7, 8, 20, 22, 51, 52, 54, 56, 57, 60, 61, 66, 161, 165, 275, 277*
hatamoto,
  See samurai,
health care, *18, 20, 22, 23, 25, 60, 61, 174, 181, 243, 245, 246, 247, 250*
Hillel, Rabbi, *283*
Hinduism, *234*
hineni (here I am), *128*
Holt, A-lan, *292*
hooks, bell, *16, 72, 74, 83*

I
Ichi-go, Ichi-e (one moment, one meeting), *10, 11, 13, 15*
Ieyasu, Tokugawa, *40*
indigenous peoples, *51*
Invisible Man (Ellison), *85*
Islam, *234*
itadakimasu (I gratefully receive), *232*

J
James, William, *96, 286*
Japan, *20, 22, 54, 72, 88, 89, 99, 101, 116, 118, 178, 180, 193, 195, 197, 198, 200, 202, 204, 206, 207, 229, 230, 232, 265, 268, 270, 272, 273*
Jibun (self), *270*
Jiro Dreams of Sushi (Gelb), *101*
Jobs, Steve, *96, 98, 99, 103*
Judaism, *234, 283*
Jung, Carl, *170, 215*

K
Kabat-Zinn, Jon, *294*
Kalanithi, Paul, *193*
kanji (characters), *15, 72, 163, 233, 268, 273, 280*
kansha (gratitude), *233*
Katz, Richard, *20, 51, 52, 54*

Ki (healing energy), *23, 25*
kiku (listen), *163, 165*
King, Martin Luther Jr., *213, 285*
kintsugi (art form of imperfection), *47, 49*
Kyoto, Japan, *35*

L

Lennon, John, *25*
  'Beautiful Boy', *25*
Levy, David M., *39*
  Mindful Tech, *39*
Life-Works program, *63, 64*
listening,
  active, *171, 173, 174, 176*
  American culture, *180*
  community, *139, 178, 180, 181, 183, 185*
  empathy, *23, 134, 141, 153, 155, 156, 158, 160, 161, 165, 166, 168, 170, 171, 173, 174, 176, 178, 180, 181, 183, 185*
  exercises, *187*
  heartfulness, *76, 160, 161, 163, 165, 170, 171, 173, 174, 180, 183, 185*
  leadership, *183, 185*
  learning, *5, 7, 20, 64, 74, 111, 165, 166*
  parenting, *29, 30, 176, 178*
  storytelling, *180, 181*
Lorde, Audre, *79, 278*
loving-kindness, *111, 273, 286*

M

ma (empty space), *178*
Malcolm X, The Autobiography of Malcolm X, *85*
Mandela, Nelson, *131, 133*
Matsuyama, Japan, *89*
MBSR, See Mindfulness Based Stress Reduction,
meditations,

Meyers, Yoshiko, *153, 155, 156, 158, 160, 161, 185*

mindfulness,
acceptance, *44, 46*
attention, *7, 8*
authenticity, *111*
beginner's mind, *34, 35, 36*
community, *121, 123, 124*
compassion, *1, 15, 18, 25, 27, 36, 47, 69, 71, 88, 104, 123, 124, 134, 136, 138, 139, 141, 146, 148, 156, 158, 160, 161, 163, 174, 185, 198, 206, 212, 213, 217, 219, 241, 243, 270, 273, 275, 285, 286, 290, 292, 294, 298*
diversity, *10, 11, 13, 22, 23, 42, 44, 46, 49, 56, 57, 60, 61, 96, 116, 118, 120, 121, 126, 129, 131, 133*
health care, *18, 20, 22, 23, 25, 60, 61, 243, 245, 246, 247, 250*
leadership, *30, 32, 34*
parenting, *25, 27, 29, 30*
psychology, *16, 18, 20, 22, 23, 25, 27, 51, 52, 54, 56, 57, 60, 61, 63, 64, 66, 67, 69, 72, 96, 101, 106, 108, 110, 111, 124, 136, 161, 171, 197, 198, 219, 220, 236, 238, 240, 241, 243, 251, 255, 273, 286, 288, 290*
respect, *27, 29, 30, 47, 49, 54, 74, 76, 124, 126, 128, 129, 131, 141, 148, 170, 171, 173, 174, 183, 202, 206, 220, 226, 258*
social justice, *292, 293, 294, 296, 298, 299*
storytelling,
vulnerability, *44, 46, 47, 49, 51, 52, 54, 56, 57, 60, 61, 66, 67, 69, 71*

Mindfulness Based Stress Reduction, *25*

Mindful Tech (Levy), *39*

Miss Universe contest, *143*

Mitsufuji, Hidehiko, *20*

Miyamoto, Ariana, *143*

mono no aware (sadness in awareness of transcience), *47*
Morimoto, Kiyo, *20, 22, 165, 166, 193, 195, 197*
Morita, Shoma, *215, 217, 219, 220*
Morita Therapy, *204, 206, 215, 217, 219, 220*
mottainai (aversion to waste), *232*
Murphy-Shigematsu, Stephen When Half Is Whole: Multiethnic Asian American Identities, *106*
mushin (no heart), *49*

N
Naikan Therapy, *204, 206, 236, 238, 240, 241, 243*
namaste (I bow to the divine in you), *128*
'Nana-Korobi, Ya-Oki' ('Fall seven times, get up eight'), *200*
Native Son (Wright), *85*
Nazis, *192*
Niebuhr, Reinhold, *207, 208*
ninjo (human feeling), *272, 273*
Nitobe, Inazo, *268, 270*
Nobel Peace Prize, *138*
nosotros (we; all of us), *129*
Nouwen, Henri, *180*

O
Obama, Michelle, *226*
okagesama de (gratitude to others), *232*
Ono, Jiro, *101*
Ototake, Hirotada, *141, 143*

P
Parker, Pat, *113, 126*
Pearce, Barnett, *245*
Pierce, Chester, *20, 56, 57, 60, 61*

powell, john a., *281, 286*
Presley, Elvis, *81*

Q
qigong, *10, 54*

R
Ram Dass, *212, 213, 298*
Rogers, Carl, *110, 171, 219, 220*
Rolling Stones, *223*
Roxbury, Massachusetts, *60, 61*
Rumi, *178, 188*

S
sabi (fleeting nature of beauty), *46, 47*
sabishii (lonely), *46*
samurai, *44, 83, 88, 116, 250, 270*
Sato, Isao, *204*
sawubona (I see you), *128*
Second World War, *193, 195, 197*
sensei (teacher), *71, 72, 74, 76*
Serenity Prayer, *207, 208, 211, 213, 215, 217*
service,
  community, *101, 111, 270, 272, 273, 281*
  exercises, *302*
  fear, *278, 280*
  heartfulness, *138, 280, 281, 292, 293, 294, 296, 298, 299, 300*
  leadership, *283, 285, 286, 288, 290, 292, 293, 294, 296, 298, 299, 300*
  loyalty, *268, 270, 272, 273*
  responsibility, *275, 277, 278, 280, 281, 286, 288, 290, 292*
  suffering, *275, 277*
Shaw, George Bernard, *286*
shikata ga nai (nothing can be done), *44, 153, 193, 195, 197, 202, 208, 215*
South Africa, *131, 133*
Stanford University, *11, 60, 61, 66, 96, 108, 277, 278, 292, 293*

Steindl-Rast, Br. David, *256, 258*
Stenzel, Ana, *29, 243, 245*
Suzuki, Shunryu, *1, 155*

T
Taoism, *207*
Taurog, Norman, Blue Hawaii, *81*
Temptations, *85*
Thatchenkery, Toto, *251*
Thich Nhat Hanh, *151, 185*
Tibet, *234*
Tokuda, Tsutomo, *20, 23, 25*
Tokyo, Japan, *46, 88, 246, 265*

U
Ueshiba, Morihei, *141*
United Nations, *138, 288*
United States, armed forces, *30, 32, 34, 133, 193, 293*
internment camps, *195, 197*

V
VUCA, See Vulnerability, Understanding, Connectedness, and Agility (VUCA),
vulnerability,
authenticity, *34, 35*
education, *51, 52, 54, 56, 57, 60, 61, 63, 64, 66, 67, 69*
empathy, *13, 25, 52, 54, 56, 57, 60, 61, 74, 76*
exercises, *78*
heartfulness, *13, 25, 34, 35, 54, 56, 74, 76, 139, 198, 259, 270*
helplessness, xii, *42, 44*
Japanese culture, *46, 47, 49, 51*
parenting, *69, 71*
power, *54, 56*
psychology, *51, 52, 54, 56, 57, 60, 61*

teaching, *61, 63, 64, 66, 67, 69, 71, 72, 74, 76*
Vulnerability, Understanding, Connectedness, and Agility (VUCA), *32, 34*

W

wabi sabi (absence of materials and material concerns), *47, 49, 74, 76*
Wakayama, Japan, *193*
West, Cornel, *280*
When Half Is Whole: Multiethnic Asian American Identities (Murphy-Shigematsu), *106*
Wright, Richard, Native Son, *85*

Y

Yoshimoto, Ishin, *236*

Z

Zajonc, Arthur, *16*

Zen, *5, 54, 67, 69, 72, 111, 185, 204, 206, 215*

www.ingramcontent.com/pod-product-compliance
Lightning Source LLC
Chambersburg PA
CBHW011742220426
43665CB00023B/2899